English Water Gardens

English Water Gardens

Guy Cooper • Gordon Taylor • Clive Boursnell

Foreword by Sir Geoffrey Jellicoe

Little, Brown and Company
Boston   Toronto

Library of Congress Catalog Card No. 87–80553

Printed in Italy
half-title Water lilies at Burnby Hall, Humberside
title page Raby Castle, County Durham.

⇉ **Contents** ⇇

❧Foreword❧

by Sir Geoffrey Jellicoe

'Studley Royal. . . . exemplifies an eighteenth-
century philosophy that Nature was barbaric
and was only beautiful or reasonable when it
was directed by Man.'

(see page 48)

How neatly this single sentence separates the past from the present. That nature is
barbaric, yes; to claim that she is not beautiful is intolerable. Consider only the light on
mountain waterfalls and rivulets, on waves breaking on the sea-shore, or on ripples on a
troubled pond. Has not our own sense of beauty been created and fashioned by nature
itself? No, we reject this one-track minded philosophy of the eighteenth century, but we *do*
accept that nature can be reasoned with, groomed in terms of civilization and made even
more beautiful to human eyes than it can make itself. This is the theme of this attractive
book.

First, the fountain. Historically, the story in social terms begins with the ordered rows of
jets in the Mughal gardens, working like page-boys to cool the air above the stately canal,
and it reaches its climax in those elegant fountains of Versailles, depicted by Rigaud,
reminiscent of a lady of fashion at the court of the Sun King. England has never achieved
such magnificence, but owing to the invention of the electric pump, little garden fountains
like sprites are popping up everywhere, fragmenting water into a thousand sparkling
diamonds, crystal chandeliers turned upside down. Further ingenious developments
allow water jets a yard or so long to leap out of the ground, spring through the air in a
graceful arc, and just as suddenly disappear from view.

Rills and cascades. The rill, usually a straight line, originated in the irrigation channel
of the Middle East and transformed itself into the symbolic channels of the Persian
Paradise garden and later the gardens of Islam. It is perhaps the supreme example of how
philosophy can lift the commonplace into the sublime. The formal cascade at Chatsworth
is a triumph of man's mastery over the forces of nature. Yet how splendid also, as the
authors of this book describe, is the cascade made in imitation of nature, whose hidden

Hever Castle
Kent

*A late autumn view of the
35-acre lake.*

order informs the disordered rocks over which waters so spectacularly break and foam. This belongs more to our own age.

Ponds, pools and lakes. At first glance these are static and contemplative, reflecting the sky and bringing the heavens to earth. But do not imagine that a stretch of water is only a reflection of the sky and surrounding scenery for beneath the surface lies a living world as vast and even more mysterious than the earthly one. He who contemplates a lake as a projection of his own subconscious will, if so inclined, meditate also upon the existence of other worlds beyond the eye; in the Zen gardens of Japan, water, rocks and gravel are laid out in intricate arrangements conducive to contemplation of the infinity of time and space.

The appeal of water is universal and immediate; it is both relaxing and exhilarating and I think it can be said that every feature in this book will give pleasure. The grouping under subjects means that you return more than once to the same garden, but this is no disadvantage for it shows that a garden can have many facets. But enough of my comments, for it is time to turn to this charming and discriminating work itself.

With magic wand still tame th' uncultur'd ground,
And bid elysian beauties bloom around;
Let scene improve on scene, and grace on grace,
Inchanting Nature dwell in every place;
Here from dry rocks, like Moses at a blow,
Command the cool translucent streams to flow,
And smoothly glide — till they impeded rise,
And with new water-falls the vales surprize,
The Chinese bridge in semi-circles fling,
Across the living streams, that widening spring;
Bounded by Alder, Beech and Poplar shades,
And facing full the falls of loud cascades,
Whose sparkling streams at intervals are seen,
Shine thro' the shades, and purl along the green,
Thro' rural elegance still winding rove,
Till murmuring lost in some romantic grove.

Anonymous (*The Rise and Progress of the Present Taste in
Planting Parks, Pleasure Grounds, Gardens, Etc,* 1767)

⇢Introduction⇠

'If there is heaven on earth it is here,
it is here, it is here.'
(An inscription on the wall of a sixteenth-century Mughal garden)

Water in a garden, whether still or moving, refreshes the spirits and soothes the senses. It was an important element in the gardens of Assyria, ancient Egypt, Persia, China and Japan, the Roman and Moorish empires, Renaissance Italy and seventeenth-century France. And it has played a part in English gardens throughout their history, from the cloisters of medieval monasteries and the *pleasaunces* of castles to the grandest of twentieth-century designs.

Significantly, the first recorded gardens were cultivated in parts of the world where water was scarce: the Islamic gardening tradition was based on the necessity of conserving water for both practical and aesthetic purposes. In Italy water was much more freely available, and it was the Romans who first used it extensively in the elaborate gardens of the early Roman empire. All of these disappeared during the Dark Ages, and it was only in the fifteenth century that the Italians started to create gardens again, incorporating in many of them superb water features which have influenced all European garden design to the present day. Before the mechanics of pumping water uphill had been perfected, gardens were often sited on hills with a source or head of water near the top: as it fell through a series of cascades and pools the water produced sufficient power to work fountains, which could grow in size as the water gained momentum. The most magnificent example of this is at the Villa d'Este at Tivoli, where unlimited water was provided by a conduit from the River Aniene, and was used for countless features, including the legendary water organ. The fountains at the Peterhof Palace near Leningrad and the waterworks at Chatsworth in England are two other fabulous examples. In many other Italian villa gardens water powered mechanical devices such as singing birds or moving animals, and was often used for *giochi d'acqua*, water-games or water-jokes, which used hidden jets to soak the unwary visitor.

Italian designers were aware that water could be incorporated in a garden in two quite different ways, which still form the basis of its use today. The first concentrated on the

The eighteenth-century bridge designed by James Paine which spans the River Derwent at Chatsworth.

Chatsworth from the Cascade Temple.

different effects that can be achieved with falling or moving water, and the second used still water as a mirror to reflect the sky and the surrounding landscape.

In seventeenth-century England the large-scale use of water for decorative purposes depended for its inspiration on the Continental ideas that were most fully developed by André le Nôtre for Louis XIV at Versailles. Just as the palace grew to be the magnificent symbol of the Sun King's court, so Le Nôtre altered and disciplined the surrounding landscape so that it too seemed to obey the wishes of the king. Immense straight avenues were cut through the forests, providing vistas to the horizon, and this grand design was complemented by canals, pools and fountains of immense size and majesty. The taming of nature on such a scale spurred the competitive aspirations of kings and princes in the succeeding century, and echoes of its design can still be seen in the gardens of palaces throughout Europe.

Le Nôtre faced a major problem at Versailles, however, where the terrain is flat and water could not be moved by gravity. Many hydraulic engineers were called in to try and solve the problem, but none managed it successfully. When the king made his progress through the gardens messengers had to be sent in advance to warn of his approach so that the fountains he was about to pass could be turned on and those already visited turned off.

At Chatsworth, one of the most magnificent houses in England, with a garden as grand and expansive as such a house demands, water is used in almost every possible variation and on a tremendous scale. It is provided by a series of lakes at the top of a slope to the east of the house, which is steep enough to produce sufficient force for all the water features.

Virtually nothing remains of the Elizabethan house and gardens at Chatsworth, which were pulled down by the first Duke of Devonshire between 1686 and 1707 and replaced with the house we see today. A few elements of the seventeenth-century landscape remain and the various dukes have been prescient enough to keep the best features from every fashion of landscape design from the seventeenth to the twentieth century. The first duke wanted his gardens to match his house and employed Grillet, a pupil of Le Nôtre, to design the extraordinary cascade on the hill to the east of the house. The water falls as a continuous carpet over sixty steps in twenty-four flights, and there were originally nine fountains, only one of which, the Seahorse Fountain, remains. The water reaches the

The great Cascade at Chatsworth, fed by streams on the moors above the house.

The Cascade Temple, built by Thomas Archer in 1701.

cascade over a wall of uneven boulders and through a pool. It is then piped underground from the Cascade Pond to a point just behind the Cascade Temple, designed by Thomas Archer in 1701, which sits majestically at the top of this great water staircase. The water rises and falls over the temple's dome, spouts through four jets in the cornice and activates further fountains in front of the temple, all of which then feed the cascade.

The fourth duke (1720–64) changed much of the formality in the gardens and employed Lancelot 'Capability' Brown to naturalize the landscape. He decided that the old house should be approached from the west, so he pulled down the old stables and offices, moved the village of Edensor and widened the River Derwent so that it would form a sufficiently imposing approach for this palatial establishment. The duke then commissioned James Paine to design a bridge in the classical style to cross the river.

The sixth or 'Bachelor' duke (1790–1858) persuaded a young gardener called Joseph Paxton, then aged twenty-three, to become head gardener at Chatsworth. This collaboration resulted in another transformation for together they built the largest conservatory then in existence. In the Lily House, the forerunner of the design for the Great Exhibition building of 1851, Paxton grew an Amazonian water lily (*Victoria amazonica*), the leaves of which can be six feet across. Beyond the Seahorse Fountain stretches the Canal Pond, 314 yards in length. At the far end from the house Paxton designed a jet of water which under full pressure can rise to a height of 290 feet, an achievement which demonstrates both his skills as an engineer and the water pressure which can be achieved naturally at Chatsworth. The jet was designed to celebrate the visit in 1844 of Tsar Nicholas, who cancelled the engagement, but it is still known as the Emperor Fountain. On rising ground to the east of the Canal Pond is the Ring Pond, surrounded by fastigiate yews and a beech hedge. The present duchess has planted two parallel curving hedges of beech which stretch southwards from this pond to encircle a statue of the sixth duke on a pillar of Sunian marble (from the Greek temple of Minerva Suniae). Above this pond are some great rocks brought to the garden by Paxton for their dramatic effect and given such names as Queen Victoria, Prince Albert and Duke of Wellington. Near them is an L-shaped pond called the Strid which is thickly planted with bamboos and other water-loving plants.

The Wellington Rock at Chatsworth.

The Willow Tree Fountain.

The Emperor Fountain of 1844.

Beyond the Strid and nearer to the Cascade is a remarkable reproduction of a fountain which may date back to M. Grillet's time: a willow tree in metal, spouting water in all directions from its copper branches. In a wood far above the site of Paxton's great conservatory, which was blown up by the ninth duke, is a grotto designed for Duchess Georgiana, the beautiful wife of the fifth duke, which is reflected in a pond of the same name immediately below it.

Water can either be used in a formal manner, leaving no doubt that its effect is entirely due to artifice, or it can be used in a way which imitates nature as closely as possible so that the visitor is seduced into believing that the flow of water exists there quite naturally and owes nothing to human ingenuity. And at Chatsworth water can be seen in all its moods: formal and naturalistic, austere and romantic, tranquil and in continuous motion. Anyone wishing to incorporate water into their garden would be well advised to visit Chatsworth, first to see how effective and revitalizing water can be, and second how it has been used by some of the most notable garden designers of their day. But whether on a major or a minor scale, water needs constant maintenance and the condition of the features at Chatsworth is a credit to the owners.

Where appropriate in this book information about the plants chosen by the owners accompanies the illustrations. Inevitably, many gardeners choose similar plants, one favourite being the most astonishing of all bog plants, *Gunnera manicata*, the leaves of which can grow up to six feet across. The plant is a native of Brazil, and bursts into full leaf over a very short period in spring, only to die back as dramatically after the first sharp frost of autumn. Among other plants in common use are *Hosta glauca, Iris kaempferi, Iris laevigata* and members of the lily family including *Hemerocallis fulva*. Possibly the most decorative and popular of all moisture-loving plants which also thrive in semi-shade are members of the primula family, including *P. japonica, P. sikkimensis, P. denticulata* and *P. alba*. Plants with architectural foliage look particularly appropriate when planted near a stream: they include *Rodgersia tabularis* and *Peltiphyllum peltatum*, the *Saxifraga peltata maxima*, and a plant only slightly less grand than gunnera, *Rheum palmatum*, the giant ornamental rhubarb.

The Ring Pond and surrounding beech hedge.

⇢Rills and Streams⇠

Old Mill House
Nottinghamshire

Though Old Mill House was constructed only in 1965, the pond and mill race were created two hundred years ago by damming the River Poulter. In the nineteenth century the fourth Duke of Portland added an irrigation dyke which crosses the river as an aqueduct, so the most interesting feature of this garden is moving water on two levels. The stone bridges are similar to those designed by Thomas Telford, who built many of England's most beautiful canals. One has the pleasure of watching the reflections of beech, ash, alder, dogwood, willow and poplar while walking on the turfed path between the upper and lower streams. Near the water's edge the planting is as natural as possible, and includes water and bog plants, ferns and water grasses. The river is stocked with brown trout, which ensure regular visitors from the heronry at Carburton Lake.

The Springs are made to run among Pebbles, and by that means taught to murmur very agreeably. They are likewise collected into a beautiful Lake, that is inhabited by a Couple of Swans, and empties it self by a little Rivulet which runs through a green Meadow, and is known in the Family by the Name of *The Purling Stream.*

Joseph Addison: *The Spectator,* 1711

There are few features more appealing than a small natural watercourse, whether it be a brook at the bottom of a cottage garden, a tributary stream of a river below a manor house, or a rill formed by the outflow from a lake in a large-scale garden or park. The now indigenous plants that grow along their margins are among the most interesting foreign introductions of the past hundred years. Care should be taken in the selection and placing of plants, and in the clearing of streams and improvement of banks, so that the result looks as natural as possible. The authors have found that an informal answer is to simplify a stream and let it colonize. Over several years their Somerset garden became steadily simpler and less labour-intensive. On the near side of the stream were a pretty but intransigent stand of comfrey, some forms of the large yellow daisy, inula, two old apple trees, up one of which grew the white *Rosa longicuspis,* and a grove of nine alder trees near the water. Spanning the stream was a red Chinese-style bridge with fretwork sides, based on the Ming 'scholar's brush-handle' design; next to it grew gunnera. A ten-inch trout was once spotted above it, and water hens and coots nested below it. Deadly aconite (*Aconitum napellus*) lived on the far bank, among ivy and hedgerow plants. Daffodils had been planted on both banks, but those on the far bank were meagre if the rampsons or wild garlic (*Allium ursinum*) had a good early start in the spring. One of the best sights of all was the red and yellow stalks of the cornus on the far bank near the red bridge, through the boughs of cool pink and white apple blossom on the near bank.

The borders and margins of streams and rills would seem to be obvious places in which to plant moisture-loving species, but such plants need a constant supply of water, and if a stream or rill drains too quickly or sharply then some form of auxiliary watering system may be necessary.

Cornwell Manor
Oxfordshire

The stream that provides the water for this nine-acre garden in the northern Cotswolds starts as a spring above the village and flows – at such a rate that it never freezes – along a course which eventually takes it into the River Evenlode. Sir Clough Williams-Ellis, the architect of Portmeirion fame, originally began to landscape the water into a series of gardens with canals and rock and bog features for a rich American woman, Mrs Anthony Gillson, in 1937.

The water tumbles through the rockery pools to a series of lakes in a woodland setting, where tall clumps of goat's beard (Aruncus dioicus), purple loosestrife (Lythrum salicaria) and the yellow flag iris (Iris pseudoacorus) thrive. Over the last ten years extensive replanting has been carried out with water-loving and bog plants such as aruncus, rheum and gunnera.

Cornwell Manor
Oxfordshire

The stream has been formalized into a higher and lower canal, both edged with stone. In the lower one is a reproduction of an Italian fountain, with the intertwined tails of two dolphins supporting a shell dish and a cupid. Such fountain statuary can now be found in every size and every sort of unsuitable material in countless garden centres, but here, in stone and on the right scale, it is a pretty central feature for the stream.

Cragside House
Northumberland

Richard Norman Shaw built Cragside between 1864 and 1895 for the first Lord Armstrong, who had made a vast fortune from the manufacture of hydraulic machinery and armaments. The gabled and castellated house, the first in the world to be lit by electricity generated by water power, is surrounded by gardens sloping away to lakes fed by rushing woodland streams.

Newburgh Priory
North Yorkshire

An Augustinian priory was built on this site in 1145 and the remains of the original stew-ponds are still evident. In front of the house is a lake made in 1780, and the entrance drive is bordered by huge yews in the shape of an earl's coronet, recalling the last Earl Fauconberg who died in 1803. The late Captain V. M. Wombwell created the splendid wild water garden on a sloping hillside above the house in 1938, landscaping a natural stream to flow over small waterfalls into a series of ponds. These he bordered with rhododendrons, azaleas, bamboos, astilbes and acers in variety, together with the weeping autumn-flowering cherry (Prunus subhirtella autumnalis pendula), the blue Colorado spruce (Picea pungens glauca) and the low-growing juniper (Juniperis horizontalis repens). The planting was chosen to give as much variation of texture, colour and shape as possible.

The Grange
Wiltshire

The Grange is a small Queen Anne farmhouse which was bought by the portrait painter John Merton in 1942. His energies created the garden that we see today. The house had been built on a spit of shingle in the middle of a water meadow, but nevertheless was never flooded. Mr Merton built two weirs and redirected the stream, which now traces a serpentine course through grassed concrete banks, the shuttering for which he made himself. Much of the original clearing of the stream was done at the end of the war by a team of military research experts freed from their official duties while waiting to be demobilized: a constructive occupation for military personnel. Brown trout and pike are sometimes seen in this stream on their way through the waters of the Grange before returning to the nearby River Avon.

Rousham House
Oxfordshire

The name of William Kent
(1685–1748) is uniquely
associated with the landscape at
Rousham, for it remains
unaltered since he was
employed to naturalize the
formal gardens laid out at the
beginning of the eighteenth
century by Charles Bridgeman
(d. 1738), designer of Stowe and
gardener to George II. The site
was propitious, having many
changes of level and being
bounded by two curves of the
River Cherwell. By altering
Bridgeman's layout Kent was
able to design a garden full of
surprises, particularly if you
follow his intended path. One of
the most enchanting homages to
an ancient Roman garden is the
rill, or Watery Walk, which
leads in a serpentine course
from the Octagon Pond in
Venus's Vale to the Cold Bath,
and thence to a rustic Doric
temple called Townesend's
Building. The sound of running
water in this grove can hardly
fail to conjure up nymphs and
shepherds, which is just what its
creator intended.

Coton Manor
Northamptonshire

Coton Manor was mentioned in
the Domesday Book, but the
present house and gardens are
the creation of Mr and Mrs
Bryant, who bought the
property in 1925. The site is
ideally suited for the display of
a large selection of water and
bog plants, and the present
owners have considerably added
to the varieties that thrive here.
Water is a major feature, and
the main stream flows from a
pond below the house to an
informal water garden. The
stream is bounded by evergreen
shrubs and encourages the
prolific growth of ferns. Spring is
heralded by the pink flowers of
the umbrella plant
(Peltiphyllum peltatum), which
show before its giant leaves,
many types of primula, the
skunk cabbage (Lysichitum
americanum), sweet-scented
azaleas and astilbes, and later
in the summer Kirengeshoma
koreana, Campanula lactiflora
caerulea, Cautleya robusta and
many forms of hosta, including
H. albo-marginata.

Dallam Tower
Cumbria

The Tryon-Wilsons and their family seat date back to the thirteenth century, but the present house is Georgian. The garden demonstrates the many different styles of landscaping that have been fashionable over the centuries. Beside the kitchen garden a stream wanders through a narrow defile to a Japanese garden designed by Hayes of Ambleside. The water then flows over a sloping outcrop of blackened limestone in gentle cascades to a pool above the lawns in front of the house. Part of the planting scheme of the 1930s includes low-growing red and golden maples, dwarf conifers, irises and moisture-loving plants: adder's tongue (ophioglossum) and the spleenwort ferns (asplenium).

To the north of Dallam Tower is a ha-ha connecting the terrace with the surrounding woodland, in which a heronry was established in 1726. The trees are ancient limes, possibly Elizabethan, and at the top of the wood is a piece of masonry which is all that remains of a house that burned down in 1236. A path leads down beside the abandoned kitchen garden and over a little stream into a pinetum. The stream is bridged in two places by Japanese-style bridges. Such a foreign importation might seem strange, but within the eclectic gardens at Dallam, which have evolved over hundreds of years, reflecting the changing fantasies of its owners, few garden features seem out of place.

Epwell Mill
Oxfordshire

The earliest surviving mention of Epwell Mill is in the records of Bruern Abbey for 1217. It was the first of seventeen water-mills once fed by the spring at Epwell. The present garden has been created by the owner around the now disused water-mill. As it descends, the stream fills three pools and finally flows into a round pond with a central fountain. The planting along the stream includes Rheum palmatum, *the pink-flowered* Rodgersia aesculifolia, Hosta fortunei, H. albomarginata, Gunnera chilenis, *an orange or yellow form of Welsh poppy (*Meconopsis cambrica*), the blue Himalayan poppy (*Meconopsis betonicifolia*), and a profusion of candelabra primulas. At another point on the stream there is a particularly pleasing group of planting which includes cultivars of candelabra primulas, astilbes, monkey flowers (*Mimulus luteus*), goat's beard (*Aruncus dioicus*) and a large-leafed ornamental rhubarb (*rheum*).*

Morland House
Cumbria

The gardens at Morland House were created in the 1870s by Lieutenant-Colonel Francis Markham around a beck, a waterfall and a quarry. The quarry was originally laid out with formal beds but is now an informal rock garden. The beck, which is about twenty feet wide, enters the garden over a waterfall and under a stone bridge. It then flows between stepping stones and over two smaller waterfalls before passing under a wooden bridge. From this vantage point one can glance upstream towards meadows filled in spring and summer with daffodils, cow parsley and May apple. Downstream the head of water created by cascades over three small dams was sufficient to drive the mill wheel and also to operate a water ram. Used to pump the spring water up to the house, this was known locally as the Squire's Well and, unused for thirty years, it has now been restored.

Little Durnford Manor
Wiltshire

The history of Little Durnford is one of continual re-creation. The north front of the manor is all that remains from the seventeenth century. Wiltshire brick and flint chequerboard were used for the exquisite eighteenth-century house, the Palladian design of which is thought to have been influenced by that of nearby Wilton. The rockery and its ponds were made in 1978 according to the designs of the head gardener from an area that used to be a chicken run, whose old pillars were retained as features. Among the plants along the watercourse are thrift or sea pink (Armeria maritima), Cotoneaster horizontalis, winter hazel (Corydalis lutea), Korean fir (Abies koreana), Bowles' golden rush (Carex riparia), bog bean (Menyanthes trifoliata), Pontederia cordata, Mimulus luteus 'A. T. Johnson', Scirpus palustris 'Zebrinus' and Iris pallida 'Variegata'.

Algars Manor
Avon

There are two bridges across the mill stream at Algars Manor, both built by the owners who have developed the water garden over the last thirty-five years. One is a working bridge to carry lawnmowers across the stream, and the other is much more picturesque. Built on the cantilever principle, it is oriental in style, and resembles the bridges found on old Chinese willow-pattern plates. In the foreground is one of the most prolific and sweetly scented of the wild water-margin or bog plants, meadow sweet or queen of the meadows (Filipendula ulmaria).

The Isabella Plantation, Richmond Park
Greater London

The Isabella Plantation, a woodland garden of about forty acres at the southern end of Richmond Park, was started in the late 1940s. The original intention of the gardeners was to plant informally along the only stream, but this scheme was greatly extended through the inspiration of George Thompson, Superintendent from 1951 to 1971. He recalls how he plotted the course of one stream with a ball of twine which unwound behind him as he crawled through the undergrowth. Though its shape has been determined by the natural lie of the land, the plantation is always changing, and it gives visitors an excellent opportunity to see a large selection of trees, shrubs and water plants. There are groups of many varieties of rhododendron, camellia and magnolia and several cultivars of Japanese azalea.

The profusion of water plants includes Primula japonica, *a cultivated form of candelabra primula. These waters attract many kingfishers and other water-loving birds. The plantation is meant to give the impression of being completely natural but, as in all wilderness gardens, a great deal of attention and skill is required to maintain that aura of careless informality.*

Upton House
Warwickshire

The second Lord Bearsted bought Upton House in 1927, and transformed it to the designs of the fashionable architect Morley-Horder, though the layout of the garden may date back to 1695 when the house was built by Sir Rushout Cullen. From the south front there is a panoramic view of a large, gently rising meadow crowned by distant elms. In between, however, is a splendid surprise – a deep, secret valley with terraced slopes leading down to a stream that has been dammed to form three rectangular ponds. Herbaceous borders flank the path leading to the pond at the foot of the terraces, and they are brilliant with varieties of phlox, geum, delphinium, peony, anemone and erigeron.

To the west of the garden another valley opens out at right angles to the first, with three square ponds dating from the late seventeenth century; the middle one is still filled with goldfish, as it was then, the lower one is now a depression surrounded by cherry trees, and the upper one has become a bog garden with clumps of bamboo, flowering shrubs and water plants, including skunk cabbage (Lysichitum americanum), Miscanthus sinensis 'Gracillimus', Senecio tanguticus and the giant ornamental rhubarb (Rheum).

→Waterfalls and Cascades←

West Wycombe Park
Buckinghamshire

Changes of water level made the creation of a cascade at West Wycombe inevitable. In a plan dated 1752 huge rocks are shown meeting in an arch under which the waters flowed, and lapping the feet of a lead figure of a river god, probably sculpted by John Cheere, before reaching the lower stream. The arch, rocks and god disappeared long ago, and now the cascade has two water nymphs in fibreglass. The arches and plinths supporting the cascade are faced in local flint. A series of small stone pyramids stands in the upper reaches of the cascade, where the water emerges from the lake beneath four low arches. These regular obstructions greatly enhance the beauty of the flow of water by producing misty sprays which reflect the sunlight, adding visual enchantment to the sound of falling water.

. . . that object is a cascade, well broken, fierce, and picturesque; tumbling down several distinct falls, and under a rude, grotesque arch of rock, emptying itself into a part of a pool, worn into a kind of creek by the violence of the torrent.

Joseph Heely: *Letters on the Beauties of Hagley, 1777*

Whether a waterfall tumbles over a natural rock formation or cement steps, walking towards it, with the sound of the rushing water reaching a crescendo even before one sees it, arouses a feeling of delighted anticipation. The height of the fall and the volume of water are not as important as that sensation, whether it be the thunderous Niagara Falls or a trickle of water from a mossy crevice in the garden at the Palazzo Borghese in Rome. Ideally the force should be powerful enough for the water to fall clear of the hard surface behind it, allowing veils of mist full of rainbows to form in front of it.

Cascades occur naturally where a strong flow is impeded by rocks or boulders scattered along its course, and where water is shallow enough to allow the rocks to stand proud of the surface, so that the water splashes and collides around them.

The Romans used waterfalls and cascades, constructed both outside and inside grottos, to cool the air and delight the senses with their sound and movement. During the Dark Ages all such frivolities were destroyed, but cascades reappeared in formal Italian gardens in the sixteenth and seventeenth centuries. Called *catene d'acqua* (literally chains of water), they consisted of a central ramp hollowed out to contain a flow of water. These were elaborated into water staircases, as at the Villa Aldobrandini at Frascati, or large-scale sculptures, as at the Villa Lante near Viterbo, where the water flows through a long series of curved basins in the form of the limbs of a crayfish in a play on the name of the original builder, Cardinal Gambara. An even more ornate example is to be seen at the Palazzo Reale at Caserta outside Naples, built for Charles III, the Spanish King of the Neapolitans. Starting more than two miles from the palace, the water is channelled to the top of a great water staircase and drops precipitously over massive blocks of stone for a total distance of a hundred yards; it then flows into a great basin with a group of sculpture on either side, one showing Actaeon being torn apart by his hounds and the other Diana bathing with her nymphs. This is the longest and largest artificial cascade in the world.

The finest surviving example in England is at Chatsworth in Derbyshire, and lesser ones are to be seen at Bowood in Wiltshire and at West Wycombe Park, Buckinghamshire.

Using changes in water level needs considerable care, and can be done formally or informally. The English, with their inherent love of naturalism and the picturesque, tend to choose informal designs, which in practice are more difficult to achieve. Where a stream descends naturally through a valley or ravine it can be subtly altered to increase its dramatic effect, but it is almost impossible successfully to reproduce a natural scene on an artificial site. Landscape designers know that to achieve any degree of authenticity it is necessary to use enormous rocks, and that most of their volume must be submerged in soil to appear natural. Even after such expenditures of labour and effort the results often look fake, and it is perhaps better to emphasize changing water levels with a series of stepped cement and concrete walls rather than attempt slavishly to imitate nature. The eighteenth-century design for the cascade at Studley Royal in North Yorkshire is entirely artificial and yet it perfectly complements and enhances the valley through which it flows, linking the romantic ruins of Fountains Abbey at the top of the valley with the lake created at the bottom.

Hever Castle
Kent

When the first Lord Astor of Hever came here the castle was surrounded by marshy ground which frequently flooded, and one of his first tasks was to solve that problem and then to create a landscape which fitted his conception of princely Renaissance life. To the south he planted a wide rhododendron walk, at the end of which the Golden Stairs completed the prospect from the courtyard. The main feature of this informal garden is the gentle trickling of water as it is channelled over the top of a cliff and into a series of artificial ponds before flowing into the Sisters Pool, a romantic scene which looks only very slightly artificial.

Old Mill House
Nottinghamshire

The uninformed visitor looking at the waterflows at Cuckney might be persuaded that water could be made to flow uphill. The explanation is slightly simpler: it is the result of man interfering with nature and nature winning. The old mill wheel was turned by the race created by damming the River Poulter, and an irrigation dyke fed by the mill pond was dug during the nineteenth century. Sixteen years ago, after this dyke had burst its banks and flooded the surrounding farmland, it was sealed off and its waters redirected via two waterfalls to the river. One waterfall lies about halfway along and the other is at the point where the dyke was blocked off, beyond a wooden footbridge. Both are bordered by heather rockeries in an attempt to make them look as natural as possible, though they exist only to help solve a problem originally created by man's interference with nature.

The Old Silk Mill
Gloucestershire

The present mill house is believed to date from the mideighteenth century and was used for the spinning of silk thread until the end of the nineteenth century. After a period as a piano factory it became the home of actor-manager Fred Storey, who made the film Rip Van Winkle *in the garden. After 1956 the then owners, Mr and Mrs George Dicks, laid out the garden in its present form and planted many of the existing trees and shrubs. The mill pond, fed by a steeply falling tributary of the stream, lies behind the house, with heathers, primroses and daffodils round its edge. A variety of ferns also grow here, including* Dryopteris dilatata, D. cristata, D. atrata, D. Filix-mas *and* Polystichum setiferum. *The stream falls over a cascade, in front of which are* Arabis caucas-ica *and purple toadflax (*Linaria purpurea*); behind is a weeping willow (*Salix babylonica*), on the walls a Virginia creeper (*Parthenocissus quinquefolia*).*

Stowe
Buckinghamshire

The gardens at Stowe are an amalgam of the classical and the romantic. Originally they had straight vistas with temples or statues at their intersections and water neatly edged with stone. Naturalism demanded that the vistas be replaced by a sweeping landscape, with the temples masked by trees and the pools made to appear natural. The two largest water features at Stowe are the Octagon Lake and the Eleven Acre Lake. The Octagon Lake was a true octagon when planned by Sir John Vanbrugh and Charles Bridgeman, but was naturalized when the landscape was replanned in 1764. The waterfall that flows through this rustic arch is channelled under the 'Shell Bridge', designed by William Kent in about 1742. This is in fact a dam between two sections of the river in the Elysian Fields, the upper part of which was dubbed the Styx and the lower the Worthies' river for it flows in front of another of Kent's works, the Temple of British Worthies.

Studley Royal
North Yorkshire

John Aislabie altered the nature of the River Skell dramatically when he created his water gardens at Studley Royal. What had been a rushing stream was enlarged into a controlled and gentle flow. Its changes of level were regulated, and a wide, shallow waterfall was constructed at the top of the long canal which finally flows under a bridge and over another cascade into the lake. The eighteenth-century idea of 'rustic' is not ours, though the bridge above the waterfall and its attendant grotto were so described when they were built around 1732. Studley Royal is a remarkable creation: it exemplifies the eighteenth-century philosophy that Nature was barbaric, and could only be beautiful and reasonable when directed by Man. The current restoration of the gardens and waterworks shows that Nature has a way of reclaiming her own unless that strict control is maintained.

Hodnet Hall
Shropshire

A bridge with sides of wooden palings spans the narrow channel between the upper and lower lakes, where a series of waterfalls has been created over a sequence of artificially stepped rough stone walls. There is an intrinsic problem in making stone walls appear old: no-one has succeeded in re-creating the informal exuberance of a stream cascading down the side of a fell in the Lake District for example. However large the stones may be, the result is always artificial. Perhaps it is better to accept the fact that water is being made to fall artificially, and that the wall of stone is man-made. No real attempt has been made at Hodnet to suggest that the waterfalls are anything but artificial, though the effect has been softened by a mass of water plants, creating a very pleasing impression of dappled sun and rushing water.

Algars Manor
Avon

The flow of water was the essential consideration in deciding where to site the mill at Algars Manor, for the pressure had to be strong enough to turn the wheel. Here the stream flows for 200 yards through a rhododendron wood, passes under two bridges and finally runs past a natural rock formation before flowing on under the mill house, turning the wheel on its way. The constantly changing patterns of the water as it falls, and of light and shade as the sunlight plays on it, are mesmerizing.

Gaunt Mill
Oxfordshire

Gaunt Mill is first mentioned in a legal document dating from 1230. It was acquired in 1603 by Magdalen College, which sold it with twelve acres for £1,026 in 1920. It continued as a working mill until 1928, but the machinery was removed in 1943 and the wheel a few years later, so all that remained were the thick outer walls which form the nucleus of the present house. Since 1949 a beautiful garden has been created along the water's edges, for the mill site embraces two arms of the River Windrush, the old mill pond and a two-acre island. A wide, curving waterfall divides two levels of water, making a continuous long arc of movement and sound between the stillness of the upper and lower ponds. It is also a reminder to the present owners of the house that their bucolic view of water and garden was for many centuries the scene of great activity, when the mill served the neighbouring countryside.

Newstead Abbey
Nottinghamshire

When a natural watercourse is altered for either practical or aesthetic purposes it very often entails constructing a barrier to control the flow of water. When Colonel Wildman, Lord Byron's old schoolfriend who bought Newstead Abbey in 1817, decided to excavate the Garden Lake, he created a sheet of water in scale with the abbey which required the building of a weir where the lake became a stream. The passing years have dealt kindly with it, and the waterfalls now look as though they have always been there, heavily protected by overhanging trees, with large male ferns (Dryopteris Filix-mas) and maples growing right up to the falls' edge. The force of the water is strong enough to produce little eddies, which finally disperse beneath the calm surface of the lower pools.

Home Covert
Wiltshire

The streams which flow through this small valley are topographically interesting as they are just below the watershed between the east and west of England. Rising from springs in or near the Home Covert woodland, those on the side of the hill flow into the River Avon towards Bristol and those on the other side feed the River Kennet and the Thames. They flow through a garden of thirty-three acres, primarily of mixed woodland, with a six-acre greensand plateau. The water garden lies to the east, in the middle of the woods. At the highest point the stream that feeds it widens into a long narrow lake, at the end of which it plunges down a twenty-five-foot high outcrop of natural rock. This waterfall is first heard from a bridge constructed twenty feet from the top but can be seen only from a path further down the stream, in a grove of very mature bamboo, Arundinaria nitida.

Rodgersia sambucifolia, R. tabularis, R. pinnata superba, Gunnera chilensis and Hosta sieboldii are naturalized here, along with over 2,000 other species of botanical and often ornamental interest. The valley is narrow, deep and tree-covered, giving it a sense of remoteness even though it is less than a mile from a major road.

Harewood House
West Yorkshire

Harewood House was created by Robert Adam and Thomas Chippendale, and its landscape by Lancelot 'Capability' Brown. It was he who persuaded Edwin Lascelles to allow his grand new house to stand in the landscape that surrounded it, albeit tidied up and artificially naturalized, instead of in the sort of formal garden which hitherto had been accepted as the proper setting for an important country house. A thirty-acre lake was created some distance from the house, fed by a stream which flows over a wide cascade. This cascade is now surrounded by groves of rhododendrons and azaleas which give a Japanese look to this very English landscape, echoed by a nearby summerhouse in the oriental style. Also close by is a rock garden planted with primulas, astilbes, Salix alba *and both* Gunnera chilensis *and G. manicata, the leaves of which can grow to six feet across. The best view of the cascade is from the stepping stones across the stream at the bottom.*

Regent's Park
London

The land of Regent's Park was originally a royal hunting ground, created by Henry IIII. Subsequently it was leased, mainly for agricultural purposes, and it was at the beginning of the nineteenth century that the Prince Regent and his architect, John Nash, planned its grandiose future. Now the park is officially under the control of the Department of the Environment.

In the winter of 1972–3 a mass of plastic sheeting was to be seen around a lake near the formal rosebeds in Queen Mary's Garden. On its removal in the spring it was discovered that a cascade had appeared, with water flowing over some thin slabs of York stone, into a pond and under a pathway to the nearby lake, the result of surreptitious planning by members of the Parks Department. Growing here are two species of marsh marigold, Caltha leptosepala *and C. palustris 'Monstruosa',* Iris germanica *and a variegated sedge,* Carex morrowii *var.* expallida.

➤Lakes and Pavilions➤

Stourhead
Wiltshire

The landscape garden at Stourhead is probably the best-preserved example of one man's dream of an eighteenth-century English classical landscape. That man was Henry Hoare II, and though his scheme of lakes, pavilions, temples, bridges and grottoes was embellished by his descendants, it remains very largely his own creation.

No place on Earth was ere discover'd yet,
For *contemplation*, or *delight* so fit.
The *Groves*, whose curled brows shade every *Lake*.

Charles Cotton: *The Wonders of the Peake*, 1681

The lawns of eighteenth-century English parks often swept down to a lake which had been formed by damming a stream, or which had been excavated laboriously by teams of workers carting earth in baskets on their backs. Lakes were sited where they either reflected the ostentatious houses of the aristocracy or at a respectful distance, where they might form part of a suitably grandiose composition of rolling acres, trees, architecture and water.

Garden pavilions belonging to great houses were built for the views they afforded and were often used as places of retreat when feasting was over and drinking was to continue. Classical precedents, of such importance to garden design in the seventeenth and eighteenth centuries, demanded that small versions of Greek and Roman temples be placed at strategic points in the landscape. Sometimes these pavilions were on a large scale, like those built at Stourhead by Henry Hoare II or at Castle Howard by the Earl of Carlisle, but often they were of a less pretentious design and served partly practical purposes. Lakeside pavilions were used for boating and fishing and as impromptu changing rooms for swimming parties as early as the eighteenth century. But even today, however swift the stream which fills it, a lake can never be as clean or warm as a purpose-built swimming pool. They are perhaps best left simply to reflect the changing sky and to nurture drifts of water lilies, as at Burnby Hall, Humberside, home of the largest collection of water lilies in England. The most magical spectacle of a lake is possibly provided at Stourhead, when the water reflects the firework display at the end of an evening's *fête champêtre* organized by the National Trust.

Garsington Manor
Oxfordshire

Lady Ottoline Morrell, half-sister of the ninth Duke of Portland, is reputed to have walked through the garden at Garsington reading Dryden aloud to the peacocks.

    The natural pond here was transformed into a stone-edged rectangle of water large enough for the occasional boating and swimming party. At the end of it stands the Temple, the classical wooden garden house brought from the Morrells' former country house at Peppard near Henley. They had travelled extensively in Italy and the compositions of water, stone and dark foliage they had seen there influenced their planning at Garsington. The trees are mostly holm oak (Quercus ilex) and lime (Tilia x europaea). Edwardian house parties are only a memory, but the statues, some Italian, some local, elevate the garden from its English provincial origins to that noble tradition which emerged in Italy during the fifteenth century.

Little Durnford Manor
Wiltshire

The lake was an overgrown swamp when the present owner arrived in 1966. The pipe that originally fed it from a pool three-quarters of a mile away was replaced by a trench, and it took two to three years to excavate the area of the present lake. The islands in the centre, made from the accumulated debris, are reached by rustic bridges, and have proved to be ideal nesting spots for water birds. Leaks from the lake have been stopped by cutting down some invasive alders, digging ditches where necessary and using 'Betonite' compound as a sealant. The planting around the lake is mainly bamboo, Gunnera manicata, varieties of ligularia, eupatorium, astilbes, primula species and hardy ferns.

West Wycombe Park
Buckinghamshire

*Like the house, the landscape at
West Wycombe is largely the
achievement of Sir Francis
Dashwood, who succeeded to
the estate in 1728 and lived
here for the next fifty-two years.
Possibly with the help of Morise
Lewes Jolivet, he laid out a
fairly formal rococo plan which
was gradually to be naturalized
after 1770. Below the house is a
large lake fed by two streams,
one of which passes a mound on
which a Temple of Venus has
just been constructed to replace
the original temple, probably
designed by John Donowell and
completed in 1748. The new
design, with pillars encircling
the statue of Venus, was made
by Quinlan Terry in 1982. On
the far side of the lake the water
narrows to fall over a cascade
flanked by two reclining water
nymphs.*

*Above these, on an island in the
middle of the lake, floats the
Temple of Music, probably
designed as a fantastic setting
for masques and fêtes
champêtres. (Nicholas Revett's
design for this apparently
insubstantial building is kept in
the Bodleian Library, Oxford.)
Little has changed here since
the death of Sir Francis. In
1795–6 and again in 1799
Humphry Repton gave advice
which was largely ignored, and
the landscape remained as a
faded dream until in the 1960s
the present Sir Francis
embarked on a programme of
restoration with the help of the
garden designer Russell Page
and the National Trust.
Members of the Hell-Fire Club
would again feel quite at home
in this setting created by its
founding member.*

West Wycombe Park
Buckinghamshire

Sir Francis Dashwood must have loved the interplay of water, for by the time he had finished his landscaping at West Wycombe the original water source had been diverted into three small rivers and a large lake in the shape of a swan, all returning via a cascade to swell the waters of the stream. There are six bridges in this landscape, all quite different. A rather discreet one supporting a wide grass path leads from the grounds below the north front of the house to one of the three islands in the lake. This island, which has an elaborate flint-faced boathouse, served as a staging post for boats on their way to the central island, on which stands the Temple of Music. From here can also be seen the two bridges leading from the same side of the house to the Broadwalk and the newly rebuilt Temple of Venus beyond.

The Walton bridge is at its most elegant when viewed from the stream which flows under it and into the lake. The arch itself is rather high and narrow, as though its design were inspired by oriental rather than occidental traditions. When Sir Francis Dashwood started to improve his father's gardens in the 1730s he was influenced by the ideals of Alexander Pope and perhaps William Kent, which demanded that walks should lead from one set piece to another, always with a building, urn, obelisk or statue as a focal point.

Castle Howard
North Yorkshire

Castle Howard is the first and possibly the finest example of baroque architecture in England, the creation of the third Earl of Carlisle and Sir John Vanbrugh. Towards the end of his life Lord Carlisle concentrated on the two great architectural features of the gardens, Vanbrugh's Temple of the Four Winds and Hawksmoor's Mausoleum.

The Temple of the Four Winds is set on a knoll to the south-east of Wray Wood, which now hides it from the great baroque mansion. Its Ionic porticos overlook the park in all four directions, and from one of them, guarded by lead statues of two of the four winds, one looks southwards across a green sward to the South Lake. To one side is a three-arched bridge designed by Daniel Garrett in about 1740.

To the north of the house is the Great Lake, made by the fifth Earl in 1797. Hawksmoor had recommended to the third Earl that he might consider, 'how beautiful a body of water at Connysthorp would look to the north front', but more than seventy years were to elapse before work on the seventy-one-acre lake started. This impressive sheet of water now helps to prepare the visitor for the magnificence of the house and its surroundings.

Stourhead
Wiltshire

The creation of the garden at Stourhead by Henry Hoare spanned the years 1744–70. His first major undertaking was to make the lake by damming the Stour, which had formerly fed two ponds, and build a series of classical and Gothic pavilions around it. The most important of these is the Pantheon, designed by Henry Flitcroft in 1753 and originally called the Temple of Hercules after the statue by Rysbrack which it houses. It has a portico of six Corinthian columns, with closed bays, screens, a vestibule and a domed rotunda, and in effect is a scaled-down copy of the massive original in Rome.

From the Grotto the visitor is directed towards the Pantheon by a statue of a river god, possibly Tiber, pointing the way as he did for Aeneas in Virgil's Aeneid *and saying, 'Whatever spring may fill the pools which are your home, and wherever you yourself emerge in grandeur from the soil, always shall you be celebrated by me.' Another important influence on Hoare may have been Claude Lorrain's painting,* Coast View of Delos with Aeneas, *which shows a Pantheon, a bridge and temples with Doric porticos grouped together in a manner which is very similar to the way the buildings relate to each other at Stourhead. In 1762 Hoare wrote of the bridge he had built: 'a stone bridge of five arches . . . it is simple and plain. I took it from Palladio's bridge at Vicenza.'*

Kedleston Hall
Derbyshire

There has been a Curzon at Kedleston for 850 years, and it was Sir Nathaniel who replaced a house built by Smith of Warwick with a palace designed by James Paine in 1759 and completed by Robert Adam. This first and only Marquess Curzon inspired the lines:

My name is George Nathaniel Curzon
I am a most superior person.

Ideally all grand country houses should be viewed across water, so in the 1770s the River Cutler was dammed to form three lakes spanned by a bridge, from which the noble pile could be respectfully admired. Boswell and Dr Johnson exchanged the following remarks on approaching the hall:

B.   One should think, said I, that the proprietor of all this must be happy?
Dr J.   Nay, Sir, all this excludes but one evil – poverty.

Bridges have not always been constructed for purely practical reasons: at Blenheim, for instance, Sir John Vanbrugh's imposing bridge crosses a lake that he designed to give an even greater sense of grandeur when the visitor approached the Duke of Marlborough's palace. The bridge that Robert Adam designed for Sir Nathaniel Curzon at Kedleston is similar in its aspirations, for it crosses the River Cutler just at the point where it had been widened to form the three broad expanses of water which lie below the house. The bridge is just large enough for two carriages to pass each other. Its three noble arches support cast-iron balustrading, and niches added between the arches may originally have held statues. The bridge has a Roman gravitas about it which would be the first indication to visitors that they were approaching the seat of a family of ancient lineage.

Thorp Perrow
North Yorkshire

There has been a house at Thorp Perrow for centuries, but it was rebuilt between 1780 and 1800 and it is likely that this is when the large lake in front of the house was formalized and extended to 100 feet wide and more than 500 feet long. At the end is a boat-house, probably built in the late nineteenth century and still used by the Milbanke family as a base for fishing expeditions or gentle boating. The bridges were also constructed at that time.

Gardens on the other side of the house lead down to another lake, which was enlarged and naturalized during the nineteenth century, when it was given an irregular outline and two artificial islands.

Flower-filled stone urns which stood on top of the house until the turn of the century have been placed at regular intervals along the water's edge so as to line up with a long avenue cut through the arboretum on the far side of the lake. This collection of specimen trees was laid out by the late Sir Leonard Ropner forty-five years ago and has now become the finest arboretum in the north of England. To celebrate his life, his son Sir John and his family built an eye-catcher at the end of the avenue, a stone and metal reconstruction of an eighteenth-century temple, made by Crowther and erected in 1978.

Hutton-in-the-Forest
Cumbria

It is not known how long there has been a settlement on this site, one of the three principal manors in the Royal Forest of Inglewood, but some scholars associate it with the Green Knight's Castle in the Arthurian legend of Sir Gawain and the Green Knight. In every century the house has been altered, and the south front, unlike the predominantly seventeenth-century east façade facing the main courtyard, is now dominated by additions built by Salvin and Webster in the early nineteenth century. The terraces were probably laid out in the seventeenth century, and below them lie a series of ponds, the oldest of which, the Middle Pond, dates from 1740. Contemporary family records mention that this lake was intended not only to be decorative but also to produce fish for the house. To one side of the lake two cascades lead to a lower lake, which was restored in the late nineteenth century.

St Paul's Walden Bury
Hertfordshire

Although the overall design of the garden at St Paul's Walden Bury has remained unchanged since the early eighteenth century, most generations of the Bowes Lyon family have enhanced its beauty. This is particularly true of Sir David Bowes Lyon, ex-president of the Royal Horticultural Society. After his death the small Doric garden temple, designed by Sir William Chambers and originally built at Danson Park, Kent, was placed at the end of the lake. It is aligned with a long beech hedge cross-allée which is terminated at the other end by a temple by Sir James Wyatt from Copped Hall, Essex. From the allée Chambers' temple appears to be part of the formality of the overall design of the garden, but looking out from its portico the visitor sees an informal lake with a drift of roses, lupins, lilies and lilac to the right of it, the only splashes of colour permitted in this series of formal green pictures and vistas.

Stowe
Buckinghamshire

Sir Richard Temple, Viscount Cobham, engaged the most prominent landscape architects of the eighteenth century at Stowe, with the result that there are more garden buildings here than anywhere else in England. The Cobham motto was Templa Quam Dilecta, *or 'how delightful are thy temples'. There are three major Palladian bridges in England, though interestingly Palladio himself never designed the type of bridge which they purport to resemble. They are, however, based on his principles of architecture. The first was built at Wilton in 1737 and the second at Prior Park near Bath; the third is at Stowe, crossing a fairly insignificant reach of water, though one side has a good view of the Octagon Lake. It was intended more as a decorative building in the landscape than as a means of crossing the river, but it has now found a practical use as the quickest way to the tennis courts used by Stowe School.*

William Kent designed the Temple of Ancient Virtue in about 1734, to terminate the great cross-walk from the south front of the house, and also to act as the focus for the romantic landscape below it. Based on the Roman Temple of Vesta at Tivoli, though with Ionic instead of Corinthian columns, it is probably his most attractive work at Stowe. Its domed roof ensures it a dominant place in the landscape, and it is reflected in one of the narrow lakes running through Stowe's Elysian Fields.

Wallington
Northumberland

The gardens at Wallington are divided into two sections, east and west. They were started in 1737 in the style of Charles Bridgeman, and two straight-edged ponds to the west still survive as informal pools. The visitor has to cross a road to enter the eastern section of the garden, where the first pond is called the China Pond in memory of a Chinese-style pavilion that has long since disappeared. All that remains of an old walled garden further on is the wall of its northern boundary, in the middle of which is the Portico House, one of the most august gardeners' cottages in England, with a portico supported by two Doric columns and pilasters. It looks out through a dark green arcade of trees and across a lawn to a long narrow lake filled with water lilies, which extends far into the woods and reflects dappled sunlight between the trees.

Pusey House
Oxfordshire

Pusey House was built in 1748. When Mr and Mrs Michael Hornby bought it in 1935 the eighteenth-century landscape to the south was overgrown with a mass of shrubs and trees loved by the Victorians, such as laurels, yews and wellingtonias. Below them the old lake had been reduced to a trickle of water through a sea of mud. One of the first jobs was to clean it and, among other things, to allow water to flow freely again under the Chinese Chippen. bridge. As it spans the lake this beautiful bridge, probably constructed in 1745, seems to float over a carpet of water lilies. To the north, near the terrace in front of the house, are beds of shrub roses and to the south are water gardens. The one nearest the bridge contains bergenia, Iris sibirica, Lobelia cardinalis, Polygonum polystachyum *and* Gunnera manicata.

Newstead Abbey
Nottinghamshire

The series of long lakes at Newstead was originally created in the eighteenth century by damming the old mill pool of the original priory to form sheets of water now known as the Upper, the Garden and the Lower Lakes. Appropriately, the most highly cultivated areas of this landscape surround the Garden Lake, but it is from across the Upper Lake that one glimpses the first romantic view of Newstead Abbey. At one end is the west front of the old abbey church, rising to its full height but with all the tracery now gone from its great west window. Beside it stretch the rest of the priory buildings, altered and embellished by Sir John Byron when he bought the abbey in 1540, and changed again by his descendant the fourth Lord Byron in 1695. Balancing the ruined façade of the abbey on the west side is a large cedar tree, and the whole romantic composition is reflected in the Upper Lake.

Chastleton Glebe
Oxfordshire

The present owners of this typical Cotswold house dug the one-acre lake, fifteen feet deep, out of solid clay. It is now full of trout that refuse to be caught, and used to be surrounded by bulrushes that refused to be eradicated but have finally been replaced by lilies, irises, marsh marigolds, water mint, hostas, astilbes and primulas. A red Chinese-style bridge and pagoda summerhouse designed by Francis Machin offer views of the island, with its mown grass and three varieties of tree, Salix tortuosa, S. babylonica and Pyrus salicifolia pendula. To the east and west of the lake are two very young plantings which in fifteen years' time will be copses of cornus, amelanchier, salix, swamp cypress (Taxodium distichum), prunus and quercus, whitebeam (Sorbus aria) and Norway spruce (Picea abies).

Hever Castle
Kent

William Waldorf Astor, an American who became a naturalized British subject, was responsible for transforming a fairly insignificant castle into a magnificent Edwardian re-creation of a Tudor mansion. The gardens around the house were redesigned in fairly simple taste in keeping with the house, but the Edwardian need for ostentation influenced the first Lord Astor of Hever to create a series of magnificent Italianate gardens and a thirty-five acre lake. This he made by damming the River Eden: the water varies in depth from three to ten feet, and it took 800 men using six steam diggers and seven miles of railway nineteen months to complete. A grand Italianate loggia was added at one end, with a colonnaded piazza on either side. The view across the lake is tranquil, but the monumental quality and Renaissance style of the lakeside buildings are at complete variance with the sixteenth-century fairytale castle just a short distance away.

Faringdon House
Berkshire

Though Faringdon House is fairly compact by Georgian standards, its grounds contain most of the features that you would expect to find on a much larger estate: pavilions, statues, urns, ponds, fountains and a lake. In the eighteenth century lakes were usually intended to be entirely ornamental. They were often placed so that great houses would either be reflected in them or be enhanced by being viewed from a distance across a sheet of water. They were not primarily intended for fishing or even boating but merely for gentle ambles from the main house, and on to a little pavilion for refreshment and gossip. And so it is at Faringdon, where only a swathe of water lilies adds colour and texture on the near side of the lake.

Hodnet Hall
Shropshire

In a reversal of the usual situation, when the sixty acres of garden at Hodnet were laid out by the late Brigadier Heber-Percy he had three gardeners to help him, and now his son has four. It is still a very small workforce to look after one of the grandest of twentieth-century gardens. Much of its glory stems from its lakes, which stretch through the landscape over a distance of more than two miles from the house. The planting around the water is necessarily concentrated in areas within easy walking distance of the house, and consists mainly of astilbe, peltiphyllum and Gunnera manicata. Further down are naturalized clumps of daffodils; the expanses of water mirror fine stands of oaks and beeches, and from the lake there are occasional vistas through the trees to the surrounding Shropshire landscape.

Among the extraordinary wealth of plants at Hodnet are some outstanding single specimens, such as Iris kaempferi, *or Japanese iris.*

Burnby Hall
Humberside

Major P. Stewart bought Burnby Hall in 1904, and in what had been a few empty fields began the creation of a three-quarter-acre private trout lake, the Upper Water. In 1910 he excavated the half-acre Lower Water, joined to the upper lake by a cascade. In 1920 the Upper Water was doubled in size and in 1936 the trout were replaced by water lilies, for which brick-walled soil beds were constructed on the bed of the lake. By 1950 there were 5,000 plants of fifty-eight different varieties.

The gardens are now looked after by a trust in association with Stapeley Water Gardens at Nantwich, Cheshire, who use it as their showcase for water lilies, water plants and water garden maintenance. Water lilies flower most profusely in July, though the earliest appear in May and the latest in mid-September, and they need careful attention: a story is told of a woman who bought five plants for £5 at a local plant sale and ten years later had to spend £5,000 to have them eradicated from the lake in which she had planted them.

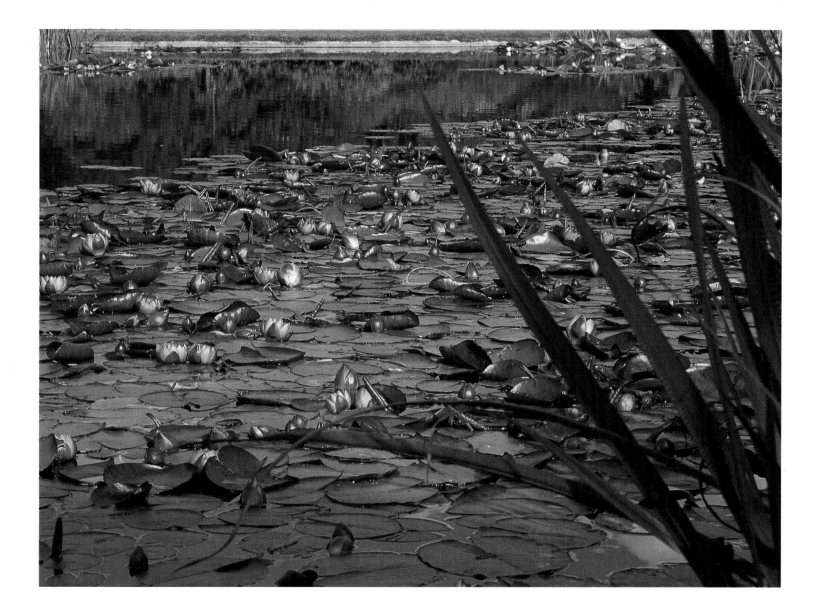

⇾Pools and Ponds⇽

Hever Castle
Kent

*At the entrance to the Italian gardens nearest to the castle is the Half-Moon Pond, which was one of Mr William Waldorf Astor's favourite spots. Like other parts of the garden it is enclosed by a high semicircular clipped yew hedge (*Taxus baccata*), which accentuates the curve of the steps leading to the pond. On the edge of the pool is a copy of the famous Capitoline Venus, a Roman statue made from the Hellenistic model derived from the Cnidian Aphrodite of Praxiteles of the mid-fourth century* BC. *She gazes down at Cupid, and they are both reflected in the water of the pool in a manner reminiscent of reflections of statues in the curved pool of the Emperor Hadrian's great ruined villa east of Rome.*

The *Ponds*, which here in double order shine,
Are some of them so large, and all so fine,
That *Neptune* in his *progress* once did please
To frolick in these *artificial Seas*;
> Charles Cotton: *The Wonders of the Peake*, 1681

Medieval religious foundations created artificial ponds in which they nurtured fish, and when the Elizabethans started designing gardens that were ornamental rather than practical, they often included pools for their decorative effect. In the seventeenth century pools became a major element in the very formal designs which were then fashionable, and their popularity was reinforced when William and Mary succeeded to the English throne and introduced the stylized Dutch tradition of formal water to English gardens.

Almost all such waterworks were swept away in the eighteenth century, when more naturalistic landscapes became popular and manicured parkland was extended right up to the front of the house. An inevitable reaction took place in the nineteenth century, when people began to want a cosier garden closer to the house. On smaller plots more intimate features were needed, and the Victorians and Edwardians added many small ponds and pools to the gardens of their villas and semis.

Until fairly recent times there were considerable technical problems. If the soil was not clay, which could be laboriously 'puddled' into the traditional watertight foundation, then it had to be lined with bricks, stone or cement, all of which were quite expensive. Then the water very easily became stagnant unless it was aerated by oxygenating water plants. Butyl rubber and rigid plastic liners have now almost eliminated the problem of leakage, and have greatly simplified both building and maintenance, and the electric recirculating pump has superseded complicated in and out flow devices and minimized the problem of stagnancy.

Modern technology has also overtaken the mills that were once found in profusion on almost every stream or river of any size in England. Many have been abandoned completely, but some have been turned into homes by people who like living on or near water and who are prepared to tolerate possible damp or even occasional flooding. The streams which once produced the power to turn mill wheels have now been tamed and redesigned, and in many cases new pools of calm water have been created along their course. The margins of these prove invaluable for gardeners who wish to extend a collection of water-loving plants, and the quiet waters may provide a home for fish, newts, snails, frogs, waterbirds and other wildlife.

The effect of a delicate Japanese bridge or a classical pavilion, like the romantic image of a swan gliding serenely on the still waters of a pool, is greatly enhanced by reflection, a fact which architects and garden designers have exploited to the full for centuries. Many of the water gardens included in this section – Hever Castle and the Dower House, Job's Mill, Bramham Park, Tatton Park, Cotton Manor and the Mill House, for example – demonstrate the ingenious use of pools and ponds as reflective surfaces, complementing both the water itself and the planting, wildlife, architecture or statuary that it mirrors.

Dower House
Wiltshire

It is thought that the pool at the Dower House was formed in the late seventeenth century; the present owners added the island in the centre in 1976. First they built a bridge to the intended spot, where they made a circle of long posts to which wire netting was attached. This was then filled with alternate layers of sticks, large stones and soil. Finally the core was covered with earth, an operation which was twice repeated to enlarge the size of the island three feet beyond the core, and to form apparently natural banks. This ancient technique for making a solid fill in water or on marshy ground was allegedly used to prepare the ground for nearby Salisbury Cathedral. The island was then planted with a willow tree and water plants. The village carpenter had built a small folly on the north side of the pool in the early 1950s, and from it one can watch waterfowl and the golden orfe that inhabit the water.

Job's Mill
Wiltshire

Once abandoned, Job's Mill has now been transformed into an idyllic small country house, half encircled by the water which once turned the mill wheel and is now enjoyed by swans and ducks. At the side of the house is a small water garden with a pond fed with water piped from the river. At the back the river has been formalized with a bridge and a small wicket gate leading to the wild woods at the side. Near the house is a small island in the middle of the river, beyond which part of the water is diverted to a waterfall and mill pond. The main part of the river, which was used to drive the wheels of the old mill, flows under the house. To the left-hand side is an expanse of lawn with shrubs behind, where one can sit and watch the changing reflections of the River Wylye. The water is at its most serene as it flows past the mill and across to a meadow where water birds strut and ruffle their plumage.

The Grange
Wiltshire

The stream diverted from the River Avon is used most imaginatively at The Grange. It is canalized, disappears under a wall and reappears again in a formal canal, which was once an insignificant narrow channel and is now six feet wide. On each side are stone platforms on which pots of conifers and white geraniums are placed during summer. The water is swift enough for trout to spawn here, and grilles at each end of the side stream prevent pike from coming into the garden and eating them. The water then flows into an old circular lily pond with an inner flint wall, and under a summerhouse designed by Lord Esher and the portrait painter John Merton, which originally had a glass panel in the floor through which one could watch the trout. Nearby are an enormous standard wisteria, the trunk of which is six inches in diameter, pink astilbes, hostas and day lilies (Hemerocallis).

Newstead Abbey
Nottinghamshire

Newstead Abbey has a romantic history. It was founded as a priory in 1170, and increased in size and importance until the dissolution of the monasteries under Henry VIII. The great abbey church is now a roofless ruin and the rest of the buildings were converted into a house over the succeeding centuries. Its most famous owner was the poet Lord Byron, who inherited the estate in 1798 and lived in the north-east wing, which contained the rooms in the best state of repair at that time. In 1817 he sold the property to Colonel Wildman, and it was he who made the large middle lake. At one end, where it narrows and curves back on itself, a footbridge has been built so that visitors may look down the whole length of the water.

The stream also feeds the Japanese water garden created in the early twentieth century, where pools are divided by large irregular stepping stones with small Japanese lanterns as focal points. The whole area is planted with conifers, including mature examples of a Japanese native, Thujopsis dolobrata variegata, maples and flourishing water plants. However, while this garden is Japanese in origin it is now over half a century old, and the formal restraint essential to maintain its true oriental character has lapsed.

Knebworth House
Hertfordshire

Knebworth House is the product of the aristocratic dreams of the Lytton family over several centuries. The present Gothick structure is the result of the medievalizing of a quarter of the house by the novelist Sir Edward Bulwer Lytton and his mother. The present owners have been set the demanding task of maintaining all this flamboyance but have slightly less of a problem with the garden. The first Lord Lytton had been Viceroy of India, and his architect son-in-law Sir Edwin Lutyens designed a pool on the garden side of the house inspired by Mughal traditions. A few water lilies float in the calm water, which is shaded by a rectangle of pleached lime trees (Tilia europaea) that add formality and height to this unusual design in the middle of a high Victorian garden.

Little Onn Hall
Staffordshire

Little Onn Hall is a grand Victorian house built near the site of an older house of which only the moat remains. In the 1890s the Misses Ashton, who then lived at Little Onn, employed Thomas H. Mawson to redesign the gardens. The original plan appears in his famous book on gardens, The Art and Craft of Garden Making, *but it was never carried out in its entirety. In 1928 Bakers of Wolverhampton laid out the area below the tennis court in a series of five lawns descending gently towards the moat. In the middle of these is a formal pool in the shape of a dog's bone, with a statue at one end and a fountain at the other. The pool is now filled with water lilies and newts. Several very large old beech trees dominate this area. The nearby moat garden, with the remains of the old manor house, has a delightfully peaceful atmosphere.*

Crabb Hall
Somerset

*Crabb Hall is a late seventeenth-century house perched on the top of a very steep slope leading to a stream that feeds an abandoned mill. The present owners have made the slope into an attractive garden with a particular emphasis on old shrub roses, lilies and silver foliage plants. A border of medicinal herbs reflects the fact that one of the owners is a doctor. Towards the base of the slope are two very old brick walls which meet at right angles, and within their embrace a lily pond has been built, with a semicircular bay on its far side. As one walks down the slope one appreciates the contrast between the still waters of the pond, patterned wih water lilies and the reflections of madonna lilies (*Lilium candidum*) and the weeping rose 'Nozome', and the gently moving stream at the bottom of the slope.*

Belcombe Court
Wiltshire

John Wood the Elder not only transformed Bath from a medieval to a Georgian town but also rebuilt some of the houses in the neighbouring countryside, including Belcombe Court in 1734. The gardens were probably laid out at the same time. The Garden Exhibition at the Victoria and Albert Museum in 1979 described them as 'a miniature Stourhead' because they contain follies, a rustic cottage, a grotto, a temple and a lake. The grotto is built of enormous rusticated stones, and through its wide-arched entrance, almost at water level, a small Doric temple can be seen on a mown grass mound not far away. John Wood was scathing about the proportions of this temple which was built by a master mason for Francis Yerbury, Belcombe's first owner, but perhaps ideas have changed for it now seems perfect for its site. It overlooks a quadrant-shaped pool about a hundred feet long, so filled with water lilies that the temple's reflection is fragmented.

York Gate
North Yorkshire

The late Robin Spencer's entry in Gardens Open to the Public in England & Wales *read, 'An owner-made and maintained garden of particular interest to the plantsman, containing an orchard with pool, an arbour, miniature pinetum, dell with stream, a Folly, nut walk, peony bed, iris borders, fern border, herb garden, summerhouse, alley, white and silver garden, two vegetable gardens and pavement maze all within one acre.' He did not exaggerate. A large wrought-iron jardinière planted with euonymus stands in a prominent position in the water garden, with primulas and other water-loving plants along the edge of the pool, which is unusual in having been built at waist height. Behind is a stone seat with a bonsai of the Atlantic blue cedar (Cedrus atlantica glauca) and a Japanese stone lantern. A seat by the pool is backed by a semicircle of clipped copper beech (Fagus sylvatica 'Cuprea'), and it is as delightful a spot as any in this multi-faceted garden.*

Barnsley House
Gloucestershire

There is much to enjoy in the gardens of Barnsley House; the laburnum walk, the formal knot garden, wide herbaceous borders, a herb garden with box hedging and a formal fruit and vegetable kitchen garden; but perhaps the most delightful place for rest and contemplation is the small eighteenth-century, Doric-columned classical temple that came from nearby Fairford Park and was rebuilt here in 1962. Sitting in the temple on a summer's evening, one is enraptured by its image reflected in the rectangular pool where goldfish flash below the surface and water lilies add texture above. Around the water grow a variety of primulas, Bergenia cordifolia, monkey flowers (Mimulus luteus), blue Iris sibirica, Japanese wine berry (Rubus phoenicolasius), New Zealand flax (Phormium tenax), roses, honeysuckles and other highly scented plants which perfume the evening air.

Dinmore Manor
Herefordshire

Dinmore Manor was originally the county headquarters of the Order of Knights Hospitallers of St John of Jerusalem, who were here from the twelfth to the mid-sixteenth century. In 1927 it was bought by the late Richard Hollins Murray, who invented the reflecting lenses known as cats' eyes. He created a fantasy of a medieval monastic sanctuary, adding a music room, cloisters with eight stained glass windows and an octagonal room with a semicircular balcony ideally placed for a lady to wave farewell to her knight. In fact it overlooks an irregular pool in the rock garden, which is filled with water lilies and bordered with many decorative acers. Beyond is the tower of the chapel of Dinmore, which dates from the thirteenth century and contains the roll of commanders of the Hospitallers, from Thomas Dunemorra in 1186 to Sir Edward Belynghom, the final commander, in 1540.

Snowshill Manor
Gloucestershire

One of the guiding principles of Charles Paget Wade (1883–1956) in designing gardens was that each turn should provide a new surprise. At Snowshill a wayward spring threatened to flood his original scheme, but finally tamed it now emerges from a pipe under the house through a satyr mask and spills into a pool in an enclosed area known as the Well Court. His design was directly influenced by a plan made by M. H. Baillie Scott in 1920, though the cross paths he suggested were replaced by paving around the pool and alongside the herbaceous borders. The pool has steps and corner pieces, and the border to the left of it is raised by retaining walls. Beyond, in the centre of a lawn, are a Venetian well-head and a high wall of Cotswold stone enclosing a niche. The garden is still planted with some mauve and blue flowering plants, which Wade considered the ideal contrast to Cotswold stone.

Bramham Park
West Yorkshire

The gardens at Bramham Park cover seventy acres and were laid out by Robert Benson, first Lord Bingley, between 1700 and 1710. They were probably inspired by André le Nôtre's designs at Versailles. The only other surviving formal gardens of a similar size in England are to be found at Melbourne Hall and St Paul's Walden Bury. Bramham owes its unchanged character mainly to reductions in family fortunes, exacerbated at the beginning of the nineteenth century by George Lane Fox, a notorious member of the Prince Regent's set.

Great vistas are laid out in various directions from the house. One includes the T-shaped canal to the south, viewed across lawns and, originally, through an avenue of beech trees. These were blown down in 1962 and have since been replaced.

The largest of the ponds is surrounded with urns and to the west of it lies an octagonal pool with one curved side.

The other main vista is along the Broadwalk, which lies parallel to the south front of the house and stretches westwards for more than five hundred yards. At its eastern end is an orangery, now a chapel, with an Ionic portico, designed by James Paine, and on the other side of the house are a series of six ponds known as the Obelisk Ponds and Cascades. Some three hundred yards beyond them is the Round Temple, possibly modelled on William Kent's design for the Temple of Ancient Virtue at Stowe. It stands on the edge of the Black Fen, a large woodland area criss-crossed with formal allées. At the foot of the six ponds is a cascade in the form of a series of terraces with steps on either side. The highest terraces are the most elaborate, and here the water issues from grotesque winged fountain masks: in the house is a charming watercolour of this feature by H. B. Ziegler.

Tatton Park
Cheshire

The opening up of Japan to British travellers in the mid-nineteenth century, and the influence of the aesthetic movement in the 1890s, inspired many people to re-create Japanese gardens at home. Lord Egerton probably produced the best and most authentic English example at Tatton, where he arranged a group of 'natural' ponds and built a tea-house, a miniature pagoda and a representation of Mount Fujiyama. Among them he planted maples and evergreens to provide a tranquil background: a golden Japanese maple (Acer palmatum japonicum 'Aureum') has matured into a very large specimen. Woolly willow (Salix lanata) and bulrushes (Scirpus tabernaemontanae) are also reflected in the water. Finally, he imported a genuine Shinto temple which he had re-erected by Japanese workmen. The temple is on an island surrounded by the Golden Brook, a recreation spot for migratory waterfowl.

The craze for things Japanese slowly grew in intensity as the nineteenth century drew to its close. The third Lord Egerton was quite tardy in his enthusiasm, as the gardens at Tatton were not laid out until 1910. The Japanese religion Shinto, or the 'way of the gods', propounds that man is on a spiritual level with trees, rocks and water. They are all considered to have a simple divinity, and nature is therefore respected. Traditional gardens are characterized by artless informality: the bridge at Tatton is extremely graceful, much helped by the delicate oval design of the balustrades. The curve in the spring of the arch is inspired by centuries of oriental design, and when the bridge is mirrored in calm waters it could be part of a composition in the spare brush-strokes of a Japanese watercolour. A branch of a conifer and a few discreet water lily leaves help to complete the picture.

Coton Manor
Northamptonshire

Decorative species of ducks, geese, cranes and even flamingos are kept at Coton Manor on a pond known as Goose Park: the main body of water flows into a long narrow stream which turns back on itself and expands into a broader pool resembling the outline of a goose. The flamingos have become naturalized and find sufficient food around the pond, though their diet is supplemented by small shrimps which form part of the food supply in their native habitat and keep their feathers pink. If the pool seems likely to freeze over, the flamingos have to be brought inside in case they break their legs in attempting to free themselves from the ice. It is good to know that there are so few problems in keeping tropical birds on a natural pool in the middle of England.

The Mill House
Oxfordshire

The old mill stands at the end of the large mill pond, which is fed by a tributary of the Thames. The walls are now smothered by Rosa filipes 'Kiftsgate', a rose of such rampant habit that it should be allowed to climb over only the stoutest walls and the strongest trees. Here, mirrored in the mill pond, it appears to form only the most benign and perfect summer curtain of beautiful scented flowers.

Hazelbury Manor
Wiltshire

Hazelbury Manor and its gardens have been transformed since the arrival of its new owner in 1972. He is involved professionally in the construction of modern industrial complexes, but his passionate interest in landscaping led him to re-create the gardens at Hazelbury and experiment with them. Conversely, the knowledge gleaned from doing so enables him to beautify and naturalize the landscapes around his building projects. In the cloister courtyard he built a small staircase and a pool fourteen feet square, using stones that blended with the old walls. Four years ago an Italian lead fountain mask was set on the staircase wall and the water flows through it into the pool, which is home to thirteen variegated Koi carp. On the walls on either side grow Clematis montana *and the evergreen C. Armandii 'Apple Blossom', and small orange trees in terracotta pots stand on the ledges of the pool.*

Rousham Park
Oxfordshire

There are few places in Britain which have not been altered by people, and the vast changes to the landscape which took place during the eighteenth century now give visitors an idealized and artificial picture of the rural landscape. William Kent created one of the earliest and most admired of English landscape gardens here, starting the change towards naturalism by softening Charles Bridgeman's square pond in Venus's Vale. Kent made the Octagonal Pond, which appears now to merge effortlessly with its surroundings. It is watched over by a statue of Venus, set above an arched cascade and protected by a pair of angry swans. The pond is full of ornamental and edible golden orfe, weighing up to three pounds, which live among drifts of water lilies.

→Statuary and Sculpture←

Rousham Park
Oxfordshire

A statue of the god Pan muses eternally at the edge of the silent pool surrounded by beech trees in the glade known as Venus's Vale.

A statue in a room challenges examination, and is to be examined critically as a statue. A statue in a garden is to be considered as one part of a scene or landskip.

William Shenstone: *Unconnected Thoughts on Gardening*. 1764

When the Italians began making gardens around their country villas in the fifteenth and sixteenth centuries they initiated a style of landscape design which has influenced the development of European gardens ever since. As their interest in classical antiquities was reawakened so sculpture became a predominant feature in their gardens. In England, Tudor and Elizabethan gardens were often decorated with elaborate trelliswork surmounted by brightly painted heraldic beasts and other grotesqueries. All these disappeared as the fashion for stone or lead statuary developed during the seventeenth and eighteenth centuries. At first statues were used as focal points where formal *allées* crossed, or as silhouettes against the sky at the end of avenues or vistas. In the eighteenth century they retreated into groves or beside informal stretches of water, gazing for ever at their reflections like the god Narcissus. During the following century half-sized reproductions appeared to lend a touch of class to suburban gardens, while ever larger and more numerous statues supported the pretensions of the newly rich. A well-placed statue can still add drama and excitement in a modern garden. There must always be a logical reason for its siting, either to terminate a vista, enhance a view or encourage the visitor to follow a particular course through a garden. Good modern sculpture is often seen to advantage in a garden, surrounded by open space where the imagination can work freely. Large pieces by Sir Henry Moore have been effectively placed beside reflecting pools where they are enhanced by the constantly changing refractions of the water. Another superb example of the perfect complementary siting of a sculpture by water is the marble relief by Ben Nicholson recently placed near a pool at Sutton Place in Surrey.

St Paul's Walden Bury
Hertfordshire

St Paul's Walden Bury is one of the very few examples of an eighteenth-century woodland garden to survive with its framework unchanged. The formal design laid out in 1725–30 was influenced by the style of André le Nôtre, and contains fourteen statues and temples, all strategically placed so that they can be seen from more than one vantage point. From the lawn below the house three wide grass allées or rides enclosed by seven-foot-high beech hedges line long vistas into the woodlands. Two of them culminate in a statue and the third leads to the church. They are intersected by cross-allées, one of which broadens out into a wide glade with a terraced theatre. At one end is a rotunda, partially enclosed by a semicircular beech hedge, and at the other, above some broad steps and a formal pool, is a copy of the famous Greek statue of a discus thrower, known to the family as 'The Running Footman'.

Iford Manor
Wiltshire

*In 1899 the architect Harold Peto bought Iford Manor, and here he was able to carry out his own ideas on garden design. In The Boke of Iford he wrote, 'Old buildings or fragments of masonry carry one's mind back to the past in a way that a garden of flowers cannot do. Gardens that are too stony are equally unsatisfactory; it is the combination of the two in just proportions which is most satisfactory.' He was influenced by the Italian tradition of garden design based on balanced compositions of terraces, broadwalks, statues and pools, though at Iford this is softened with English planting. A stream feeds a pond near the top of the hill and then descends into a semicircular pool, which is reached across a paved courtyard from the loggia at the south-east corner of the house. A river god sits on a plinth above a fountain mask which spills water into the pool. Shielding the lion is mind-your-own-business (*Helxine soleirolii*).*

Osborne Farm
Kent

Gardens nearly always reflect the personality of their owners, and sometimes they disclose their obsessions. Mrs Margaret Stace loves garden gnomes. Twenty-five years ago she found an overgrown pond in a field adjoining the farmhouse. She cleared it and at first added just a few rocks around the edge with some gnomes and lilies. They have since been joined not only by their friends and relations but also by Snow White and her Seven Dwarfs; there are now more than a hundred gnomes round the pond, some on seats, some watching the water and some gazing at the half-timbered floating duck-house. Plaster penguins and storks have appeared too, together with ducks, both in effigy and in person, among the marigolds, snapdragons, nasturtiums, geraniums and water lilies. Mrs Stace places all the figures outside in different groupings each spring and takes them inside for safekeeping every winter.

Stourhead
Wiltshire

Henry Hoare II of Stourhead was much influenced by Virgil's Aeneid, in which a sibyl warns Aeneas: 'Light is the descent into Avernus [the infernal region] but to recall thy step and issue to the upper air there is toil and there is task.' The grotto at Stourhead is intended to represent such a subterranean world. In a recess on one side is a stone bath, above which a statue of a sleeping nymph reclines on a cascade of continuously flowing springs. The nymph is a lead copy of the Sleeping Ariadne from the Belvedere Collection in the Vatican, and is immortalized in Alexander Pope's translation of a poem of the Italian Renaissance:

> Nymph of the Grot, these sacred springs I keep
> And to the murmur of these waters sleep;
> Ah! spare my slumbers, gently tread the cave,
> And drink in silence or in silence lave.

Rousham Park
Oxfordshire

The tradition of the idealized natural landscape, as represented by William Kent's design at Rousham, demanded that antique statues and temples be placed at strategic points throughout the garden to provide the visitor with echoes of ancient times, and also with places to sit and contemplate the vistas beyond the River Cherwell. The gardens contain at least fifteen statues and pavilions. A memorial to a favourite family dog is inscribed on one of the stones of the cascade:

> In front of this stone lie the Remains of
> RINGWOOD
> an otter-hound of Extraordinary Sagacity
> Tyrant of the Cherwell's Floor
> Come not near this sacred gloom,
> Nor, with thy insulting brood,
> Dare pollute my RINGWOOD's tomb . . .

Castle Howard
North Yorkshire

In 1850 the landscape architect W. A. Nesfield was asked to redesign the grounds at Castle Howard. The work included the placing of the Atlas Fountain below the south front, and in order to provide the necessary water pressure a reservoir was constructed in Wray Wood. At the same time a vista was cut into the wood, extending the line of the main approach to the north front of the house; it was to be completed with a column or obelisk in the middle of the new reservoir to balance an existing obelisk to the west. This second obelisk was never erected, but its plinth still stands ready in the reservoir, ornamented with carving rescued from one of the eighteenth-century buildings that once graced Wray Wood: just above the water level, beneath a fairly naturalistic band of images of water-loving plants and leaves, is a chorus line of fishes in bas-relief.

Sutton Place
Surrey

*The gardens at Sutton Place are
the result of the differing tastes
and ambitions of aristocrats,
newspaper owners, oil magnates
and art collectors. In 1900
Gertrude Jekyll helped Lady
Northcliffe to improve the
gardens, and some traces of her
inspiration remain in the
planting of the herbaceous
borders near the house, and in a
large irregularly shaped pond
set in a lawn some distance
away. Ben Nicholson's* White
Relief *(1937–8) was placed here
at the suggestion of the
landscape designer Sir Geoffrey
Jellicoe. It was always
Nicholson's ambition to site a
wall in a landscape and the
placing of this slab of marble,
thirty feet long and fifteen feet
high, is a triumph. The
sculpture is positioned so
exactly that its subtle changes
of plane are perfectly reflected
in the surface of the water.*

Faringdon House
Berkshire

*Statues and their siting do not
always have to be serious. These
gardens are full of the
unexpected, and nothing more
so than the statue in this pool in
front of a pretty Georgian
orangery. In the pond is a bust
of a Victorian gentleman, Sir
Henry Havelock, hero of the
Indian Mutiny. Lady Canning
wrote of him. 'Havelock is not in
fashion but all the same we
believe that he will do well. No
doubt he is fussy and tiresome
but his little old stiff figure looks
as active and fit for use as if he
were made of steel.' After
twenty-three years as a
lieutenant, Havelock died of
dysentery in 1857, the year of
the mutiny, before he knew that
he had been made a
Major-General. It is to be hoped
that he would have appreciated
his semi-submerged memorial.*

Easton Grey House
Wiltshire

Easton Grey is a beautiful eighteenth-century house in a nine-acre garden with spectacular views of the River Avon. Over the past twenty-seven years the present owner has replanted the garden extensively. There is a cruciform pool in the middle of the rose garden, a lily pond in the walled garden, and a larger round pool in the main garden with a stone seat beside it, from which there is a good view of the Avon. On the other side of the pool is the slightly more than life-size bronze statue of The Girl with the Doves, *of which David Wynne, the sculptor, says, 'The subject of this group is the joy of letting go. The girl is herself freed by releasing the birds which she had held in her arms.' The statue is set within wonderfully simple planting: low-growing juniper (*Juniperus horizontalis), *a cultivated form of bramble (*rubus), *weeping willows (*Salix babylonica) *and a* Ginkgo biloba.

Hodnet Hall
Shropshire

The gardens at Hodnet, which cover some sixty acres, are the creation of the late Brigadier A. G. W. Heber-Percy. He started them in 1922, with a basic design of a series of lakes and intensive planting. The Brigadier dammed a small stream to make the Main Pool opposite the house with its subsidiary Horse Wash Pool, which leads, via the Water Garden, through Pike Pool, Heber Pool and Paradise Pool to two further long stretches of water. Planted around the pools close to the house are many types of gunnera, primula, astilbe and fern, and behind them are large drifts of colourful rhododendrons, azaleas and primulas. In one corner of the Horse Wash Pool two life-size lead cranes have been effectively placed.

Moats and Canals

Westbury Court
Gloucestershire

The Dutch-style garden at Westbury Court was an overgrown wilderness when it was given to the National Trust in 1967, but the discovery of the 1690 account books of Maynard Colchester, its creator, which list the plants originally used, and of an engraving by Kip published in 1712, made it possible to reconstruct the original layout. Its main feature is the narrow Long Canal lined by yew hedges, with a tall brick pavilion raised on Ionic pillars at one end, exactly sited so that its full height is reflected in the still water. The pavilion also overlooks the T-shaped canal and the parterre near to it, which has been re-created as a Dutch-style cut *parterre as opposed to the more complicated French* broderie *pattern. Most of the original plantings were of a practical nature: fruit trees were trained on the walls and there was a large vegetable garden. Fish and eels were farmed in the canals.*

> In this Canal several Sorts of Fish are confin'd, as Trout, Perch, Carp, etc. of a very large Size, and tho' it is deep, yet the Water is so transparent that you may easily discover the scaley Residents, even those of smallest Dimensions: And this Canal is so very much frequented in the Summer, that the Fish will not be disturb'd at your Approach; but are almost as tame as the Swans (two whereof continually waft themselves with Grandeur in this Canal), which will not scruple to take an uncommon Feeding from your Hands.
>
> Stephen Switzer: *A Description of Dyrham Park near Bath*, 1742

An expanse of still water with calm reflections used to be a particularly English or northern European sight, in contrast to the fountains of Mediterranean countries. But now moats and canals are rare in the British landscape. Moats began to disappear in the fifteenth century, when under the new Tudor dynasty England began to enjoy more political stability, and fortified houses were no longer necessary; and the canals of sixteenth- and seventeenth-century formal gardens vanished with the arrival of naturalism in the eighteenth century.

In Britain moats have been dug for defensive purposes since before the Roman conquest. They were most often made on low-lying land and in clay, which provided an impermeable base. To be effective (against robbers as well as military assault) a moat needed to be at least thirteen feet wide and six feet deep. When they were no longer useful they were either filled in, so that house and garden could be extended in the Italian or French fashion, or they were drained and enlarged to make lakes, as at Raby Castle, County Durham. At Scotney Castle in Kent the moat was enlarged into a decorative lake on one side and the walls of the old castle ruined yet further to form a romantic eye-catcher, to be glimpsed, through a glade of rhododendrons and azaleas, from the new house on an escarpment some 300 yards away. Leeds Castle, also in Kent, appears to be the perfect example of a moated castle. The irony is that the medieval perfection we see is the result of a great deal of American money in the 1920s.

Canals probably derive from the practical aspect of monastic life – the fish- or stew-pond. When manor houses or grand country houses were built on religious foundations remnants of the stew-pond were often used decoratively in the gardens. But as a garden feature canals were never as important in England as they were in France, where one of the first to be constructed was at Fleury-en-Bière in the sixteenth century. Eight hundred metres long, it is thought to have been the model for the Grand Canal at Fontainebleau, built for François I. The genius of magnificent large-scale *allées d'eaux* and other fabulous garden waterworks was André Le Nôtre (1613–1700), who planned the splendid water parterres at Vaux-le-Vicomte and the extraordinary basins and fountains at Versailles for Louis XIV. This taming of nature was a ruthless business. At Vaux one village and two hamlets were swept aside to make room for the park; and at Versailles, victims of the swamp gases released during the initial excavations were hauled away by the cartload.

These designs would have influenced the water features in the gardens that still exist at Wrest Park (*c* 1706) in Bedfordshire and Melbourne Park (*c* 1704) in Derbyshire. Many other such gardens were swept away in the eighteenth century by William Kent and 'Capability' Brown. Much smaller-scale canals have been made since that time, though the British definitely prefer informal expanses of water to those restricted by parallel banks and edged with cut stone and a coping. Canals look best when they have the simplest stone surround or none, and the most restrained drifts of aquatic plants, if any.

Kingcombe
Gloucestershire

The house and garden at Kingcombe are the creation of Sir Gordon Russell, the distinguished furniture designer who had a considerable influence on English taste from the early 1920s until his death in 1980. The first stone of the house in the Cotswolds was laid on Boxing Day 1924 and Sir Gordon continued working on both the house and garden throughout his lifetime. He noted,

Obviously, in England fountains cannot have the same sparkle and feeling of coolness which is so necessary in a hot country but less welcome in an English November. On the other hand, we have pools and I have a small canal which takes a boat for the children and is planted with water-lilies . . .

*The ruined tower is a pseudo-medieval folly with a dungeon built by Sir Gordon at one end of the canal. Red valerian (*Centranthus ruber*), Golden elder (*Sambucus nigra 'Aurea'*) and deer fern (*Blechnum spicant*) all grow on the wall or beside the water.*

Birtsmorton Court
Worcestershire

The moat and foundations of Birtsmorton Court are thought to have been started before the Norman Conquest, but the earliest surviving part of the superstructure is a fourteenth-century archway on the north side, which may have been built by either the Nanfan or the Hakluyt family, both of whom are known to have lived here. An ancient yew tree in the grounds is said to have sheltered the young Cardinal Wolsey before his fame, fortune and disgrace at the hands of Henry VIII. But most of the court was rebuilt in 1580 on the older stone foundations, and rises dramatically out of the moat, which has been extended so that it almost forms a lake on two sides of the house.

Birtsmorton Court is splendid, romantic and hidden, encouraging a local historian to write in the early part of this century:

Although this isolated, fossilised, moated manor of olden times is of a sort to work powerfully on that superstitious feeling and credulousness which are so deeply rooted in the minds of every rural and secluded population . . . the dead who once paced those garden walls are not forgotten, and where can there be a more fitting haunt for those sights which 'we poor fools of nature' shrink from, than the spaces covered with the deep shadows of those overhanging trees?

128

Broughton Castle
Oxfordshire

For defensive purposes a moat needed to be about four yards wide: the fourteenth-century moat which surrounds Broughton Castle is wider and at least five feet deep, with a surface area of three acres. Unusually, it encloses a garden next to the castle, also of some three acres, which suggests that the moat was created as much for reasons of status as for military purposes. The house was partly rebuilt in the sixteenth century, and its mixture of architectural styles is marvellously reflected in the calm waters of the moat.

Within the castle is a walled Ladies' Garden laid out in a fleur-de-lis pattern of box hedging filled with roses. Along the outside walls of the castle are long borders, possibly planned by Gertrude Jekyll but extensively replanted since with a mixture of shrub roses and herbaceous plants. Long stretches of lawn, or meads, add to the tranquillity of the view of the castle across the still waters of the moat.

Little Onn
Staffordshire

Little Onn is mentioned in the Domesday Book as 'Anne'. The Peshall family owned the manor during the Middle Ages and built a small moated manor house about 150 yards away from the present house. Almost all of the old house has disappeared, but the moat remains, and huge ancient yews stand beside it, overhanging the water where golden orfe live. Beeches have been planted on the outside of the moat and underplanted with spring flowers: bluebells, primroses and daffodils. In one corner, just outside the moat, is a sunken formal rose garden, and a long wall encloses the kitchen garden on the north side.

Studley Royal
North Yorkshire

When John Aislabie was forced by the South Sea Bubble scandal to resign his post as Chancellor of the Exchequer in 1720 he decided to make his life's work the creation of the formal water gardens at Studley Royal. He took a wild woodland valley through which the River Skell runs and turned it into an eighteenth-century dream of Nature tamed and idealized by Man. The river was shaped into formal ponds and dragooned into canals, finally to be swollen into a lake, and miniature Greek temples were placed at vantage points: the Doric Temple of Piety overlooks the Moon Pond. This enormous circular sheet of water with a statue at its centre is flanked by two curving spandrel-shaped ponds, and all three are bounded for their entire length by the canal, which flows over a formal cascade between two Venetian fishing houses into the lake.

→Fountains and Masks←

Hever Castle
Kent

Fountains became an increasingly important element in late Victorian and Edwardian gardens, partly because of improvements in water engineering and partly because of tastes and objects acquired by the upper classes in their travels on the Continent. William Waldorf Astor was American Minister in Rome for fifteen years, during which time he collected many of the statues and ornaments which subsequently adorned the Italianate gardens at Hever; they are set in an enclosed rectangle one-eighth of a mile long, with an Italian-style loggia and two piazzas at its farthest end. Twin staircases curve down from the main façade, round a circular pool and on to a terrace overlooking the lake. They enfold a decorative fountain designed by Frith, with two nymphs gazing at the water flowing from an urn held up by putti.

The brilliant contrast of dancing, refracting jets against trees or shaded buildings gives the eye the delight that is at the root of impressionism. A single jet alone, in suitable settings — where there is a dark background for choice — has the beauty of some miraculous flower.

Gertrude Jekyll: *Garden Ornament*, 1927

The idea of forcing water through a small aperture so that it throws a spray or jet into the air is both simple and attractive. Light seen through moving water is mesmerizing, and our ancestors were prepared to go to a great deal of trouble and expense in order to produce this very pleasing artificial effect in their gardens.

The Emperor Hadrian had fountains at his famous villa east of Rome, and Pliny the Younger also mentions fountains in the descriptions of his villas. The Goths destroyed these luxuries, which nevertheless survived within monastery walls. In their gardens and cloisters the monks grew a variety of herbs for culinary and medicinal purposes. Cloisters were usually laid out in a four-square pattern with a water feature at the centre: a well-head, a small pond or — especially in southern Europe — a fountain.

The sound and sight of moving water is especially important in hot climates, as is best exemplified by the gardens that Arab invaders built in those parts of Europe that fell under their sway, of which the best-known is the Alhambra at Granada in southern Spain. In the centre of the Court of the Lions is a fountain of twelve stone lions spouting water and supporting a twelve-sided stone basin, all carved in about the eleventh century. The many other fountains in the numerous courtyards and patios of this magical palace demonstrate the Arabs' passion for, and prudence with, water.

Fountains have rarely played a significant part in English garden designs, though a notable exception is the Emperor Fountain at Chatsworth in Derbyshire, the jet of which can reach 96 yards. The fashion for fountains came and went with the creation and destruction of the formal gardens of the seventeenth century and earlier. They were not necessary to the planned naturalism of 'Capability' Brown, and there are no fountains at Stourhead. They came to Blenheim only in the 1920s, when the ninth Duke of Marlborough had some designed by Achille Duchêne. The Italianate fashion of the late nineteenth and early twentieth centuries encouraged the Edwardians to invest time and money in the creation of quite elaborate fountains, such as the Shell Fountain at Cliveden, and in municipal set pieces such as the Victoria Memorial in front of Buckingham Palace. The engineering and maintenance required by water gardens in general and fountains in particular were very problematical, however, until the invention of the electric recirculating pump in the latter part of this century.

Another form of fountain is the stone or metal spout which forces water to gush swiftly by constricting its flow through a narrow pipe. Traditionally such spouts are embellished with masks, human, animal or grotesque. Images of satyrs, fauns, ancient river or sea gods and lions are ever popular. But the most charming human representation that we have seen on a fountain mask is of Sir Gordon Russell in his garden at Kingcombe in Gloucestershire, where he is portrayed in Cotswold stone, forever spouting water, with his spectacles still on his nose.

Hever Castle
Kent

In one of the yew-hedged enclosures in the middle of these Italianate gardens is a splendid rectangular pond, on the edge of which is a slightly subdued image. Triton, son of the sea-god Poseidon, either straddling or holding a spouting dolphin. The work is attributed to the Florentine sculptor Bartolommeo Bandinelli, variously described as a pupil or rival of Michelangelo, and was sculpted in about 1550. It would naturally be at home in any classical Italian garden, but it also fits much more simply and comfortably into the English landscape than the baroque fantasies of the elaborate water display overlooking the lake.

Buscot Park
Oxfordshire

The house in Buscot Park was built in about 1780 by Edward Loveden Townsend, who probably acted as his own architect. It was bought by the first Lord Faringdon in 1889 and is still lived in by his descendants. The gardens and park stretch away to east and west, culminating in each direction in a stretch of water. To the west, below a fifteen-acre reservoir, is a bowl-shaped kitchen garden, in the middle of which is a large sunken circular pond edged with a stone balustrade. In the centre is a slightly demented, gleeful satyr holding on his shoulders a wineskin from which issues forth a stream of water. This is a fine example of a type of sunken water feature of Italian Renaissance provenance which was much favoured by the Edwardians. With some exceptions the English have not been particularly skilled at building and maintaining elaborate waterworks; the gardens at Buscot are a notable exception.

During the first decade of this century Lord Faringdon commissioned Harold Peto (1854–1933) to design a water garden 250 feet long to the east of the house; it leads to a twenty-acre lake, on the far side of which is a small temple. The water flows down through a series of shaped ponds connected by straight canals and waterfalls. In the round pond nearest to the house is a fountain showing a diving boy in the coils of a dolphin. The fountain jets provide the initial momentum for the water as it starts its flow through the pools, under the bridge and out to the lake, all shaded by the branches of an avenue of tall trees.

Castle Howard
North Yorkshire

The Atlas Fountain is the most important feature of the gardens below the south front of Castle Howard. The gardens were laid out by W. A. Nesfield and the Atlas Fountain was erected in 1853. It was designed in collaboration with John Thomas, one of the Prince Consort's favourite sculptors, who executed the five figures in Portland stone. Four of them hold up cornucopias which drench Atlas, who supports a bronze globe with gilded zodiac signs. The tazza pedestal, shells and basin were made by local masons. This remarkable creation shows another side of the imagination of Thomas, who also sculpted a famous statue now placed near Westminster Bridge called The Queen of the Eastern Britons Rousing her Subjects to Revenge, *more familiarly known as Boadicea.*

Kingcombe
Gloucestershire

After building the house at Kingcombe, Sir Gordon Russell, afterwards a Director of the Council for Industrial Design, had many discussions with Sir Geoffrey Jellicoe and his then partner, Russell Page, about the plans for the garden. A design by Jellicoe dated 1936 was never carried out in full.

Sir Gordon was fortunate in having a spring above the house which proved sufficient for all the water incidents that are now to be found here. Some of the more notable features in the garden are based on Italian ideas, one being a narrow stepped cascade beside the main staircase that leads from a yew-edged lawn down to the canal. A dramatic stone fountain mask fills a basin beside the lawn with water which is subsequently piped over the cascade.

Hidcote Manor
Gloucestershire

The gardens at Hidcote Manor, created from 1907 onwards by an American, Major Lawrence Johnston, are arguably the most influential to have been made in England this century. Their importance lies in their development of a series of garden rooms, usually divided by tall hedges, each displaying either a particular genus or a colour scheme. An ivy-clad circular pond almost fills a round garden hedged with close-cropped yew. The pond is raised, and seems on the point of overflowing because the water is kept only just below the rim. Almost the only colour here is the climbing Tropaeolum speciosum, which spreads its flame-coloured ribbons across the hedges in summer. The boy and dolphin fountain in the centre of the pond is a focal point for two of the many axial walks which divide the garden, encouraging visitors to discover its many secrets, and leading to views over the surrounding Cotswold landscape.

The Garth
Cumbria

This is the garden of an enthusiast. The suburban house was built in 1923 on a fairly steeply sloping site separated from the old town of Penrith by a modern housing development, but the water garden was not started until 1975, in what was an old pasture field. Just below the house is a formal rectangular lily pond, fifteen feet long with a small fountain in the middle. Its jet slightly masks the two irregular ponds below, which are connected by an artificial stream and small waterfalls. Planted around the higher pool are lilies, monardas (bergamot), azaleas, primulas, hostas, euphorbias and conifers. Thus, within a fairly small area a completely captivating water garden has been created.

Snowshill Manor
Gloucestershire

Snowshill Manor garden is essentially the creation of the architect Charles Paget Wade and dates from 1919: it incorporates the old farm buildings and the dovecot, and uses the spring which rises under the house to feed a series of pools and troughs. Wade maintained that the plan of a garden is more important than the flowers, and that no garden should display everything at once: instead it should be designed to have a sense of mystery. Water was a problem at the outset, and Wade noted that the spring had formed a treacherous swampy morass in what had been a cattle yard and was to be the lower garden. The spring is now piped under the house, through a satyr fountain mask designed by Eileen Cosomatti and into a stone trough before being taken under a courtyard to a large pond. It then emerges into two other small stone troughs before finally embarking on a sort of adventure trail plotted by Wade along its ancient course.

Regent's Park
London

Financial problems prevented the completion of the original plans of the Prince Regent and his architect, John Nash, for Regent's Park. Nash did succeed, however, in building the grand terraces which lie on its circumference, but he erected only eight of the large villas that he had planned. This is probably the grandest of the royal parks, and it has been enhanced by features added to it over the last century. On a lake near a garden named after the late Queen Mary the Triton Fountain has been erected. The son of Poseidon is seen here blowing a conch shell while being watched admiringly by one mermaid and with less enthusiasm by another, both of them crouched at his tail. Designed by W. McMillan, the fountain was erected to the memory of Sigismund Christian Hubert Goetze (1866–1939), painter, lover of the arts and benefactor of the park.

Faringdon House
Berkshire

The apparently conventional façade of Faringdon House, brick, five bays wide, and altogether what the Georgians would have called 'a neat villa', belies its eccentricity. For many years it was the home of the late Lord Berners, immortalized by Nancy Mitford as Lord Merlin in The Pursuit of Love. *Each spring he had his pigeons dyed green, pink, blue and yellow in order to shock and amuse his guests. But he respected the landscape that he found: the approach through the park crosses an eighteenth-century iron bridge, below which is a circular pond with a jet of water at the centre.*

Barnsley House
Gloucestershire

Rosemary Verey and her husband, the late David Verey, moved to Barnsley House in 1951, and laid out the garden together: Rosemary, a great gardener and plant-lover, filled it with choice specimens, and David was responsible in 1962 for creating a cross-allée bisecting the garden, with a temple at one end and a delightful fountain by Simon Verity at the other. The main design of this fountain, in bas-relief on spangled Purbeck stone, is inspired by the centuries-old economic importance of sheep to this part of England. Two Cotswold rams are watered by jets emerging from four Hornton stone frogs carved by Judith Verity on opposite sides of the small pool. Large clumps of Angelica archangelica, Alchemilla mollis, Ligularia clivorum 'Desdemona', hostas and tree peonies grow around the water. Wherever you are in this part of the garden your senses are tingled by the sound of the water from the fountain.

Sutton Place
Surrey

The work carried out at Sutton Place in 1980–5 by Sir Geoffrey Jellicoe for Stanley J. Seeger has been called the largest private commission since the gardens at Chatsworth were laid out in the nineteenth century. To the east of the house is the Paradise Garden. Reaching paradise is always difficult: here entry is gained by stepping stones across a moat. Curling paths suggested by the spiralling chimneys of the Tudor house divide the garden into twelve separate areas. At each of the four main intersections is a circular brick rondel with a small pool and flower-shaped fountain, bounded by niches covered in climbing roses and jasmine. The brick walls protect the garden from the hostile world, the plants fill it with colour and scent, and the sound of splashing water completes the illusion that one is in a celestial garden (traditionally the Islamic reward for all those who died fighting for the honour of the Prophet).

On the moss-covered red brick walls of the garden are a series of stone masks that spill water into shallow basins from their open mouths.

The American Museum
Avon

The American Museum was established at Claverton Manor, Bath in 1961 by Dr Dallas Pratt and the late John Judkyn to show domestic artifacts associated with North America from the mid-seventeenth to the end of the nineteenth century. The house was designed by Sir Jeffry Wyatville in about 1820, and changes to the gardens, designed by Ian McCallum, its inspired director, have continued ever since. An arboretum was started in 1979, and as the site was cleared a dell was discovered, springs were tapped on the hillside, and a cascade and a waterfall created. In another part of the grounds water trickles through a traditional lion fountain mask into a basin below a formal semicircular niche. Poet's ivy (Hedera helix 'Poetica'), ivy-leaf toadflax (Cymbalaria muralis) and the bird's nest fern (Asplenium nidus), all of which enjoy a moist atmosphere, have been encouraged to grow here.

Kingcombe
Gloucestershire

This delightful waterspout in the form of a mask in Cotswold stone depicts the owner of Kingcombe, Sir Gordon Russell, with his glasses on the end of his nose.

➢Photographic Notes➢

Soon after I began photographing water gardens for this book I found that I preferred to work from late afternoon to the last light after sunset and again from before sunrise to mid-morning. (Between the two sessions at each garden I slept in my camper bus.) I arrived at the next place in the afternoon, in time to assess both the play of light on the water and the essential character of the garden. I felt it was vital to understand the particular effect of light on each individual garden, and to study the sky and the water — the two principal elements of every image.

The sun moves across the surface of the earth one degree in every four minutes, and I cannot over stress the importance of working out a picture in detail in the mind's eye and being in position with the camera at the ready well before one needs to shoot. Setting up my camera and tripod before dawn, I have often felt an excitement at watching the sun rise and gradually move into the position which I know will provide good light on the subject, aware that the ideal conditions will have gone in five minutes.

I chose to work with a Hasselblad 6 × 6 cm, which is the largest format camera that is easily portable, anything larger being too slow, too heavy and too expensive to be practicable for the amount of work to be covered in the time available. And I found a Polaroid back invaluable in planning the final image. I used EPN 100 Ektrachrome 120 film, which is less contrasty than the 64 ASA film; it just seems to suit me, and I have absolute control over the E6 processing.

I used an 80 mm normal lens, a 50 mm wide-angle, a 150 mm telephoto and very occasionally a × 2 teleconverter, which in combination with the 150 mm lens gave me a 300 mm telephoto. I was very anxious to let the colour of light in each garden speak for itself and used filters only when the natural light needed to be pulled back from dull green or dirty blue: an 81 to 81B to give it a warm brownish quality; a 5Y or 10Y (Y = yellow) to reduce the blue; 1A to add a little pink; and once or twice I used a gradual ND (neutral density) filter to bring the exposure value of the sky closer to that of the water and landscape.

A tripod and a spirit level are essential when photographing water, a step ladder is useful, and I always take a plastic bag with me for rubbish, i.e. film wrappers etc.

All books of this nature require a good deal of co-operation from individual gardeners and garden owners, and without exception everyone I encountered welcomed me with warmth, generosity and helpfulness. It would be impossible to mention all those who deserve special thanks, and I have therefore taken a representative sweep across the country, mentioning just a few people from the different parts of England that I visited in my water garden tour in 1986:

Mrs L. Ingrams; Mr and Mrs C. Cottrell-Dormer; Dr and Mrs David Hatchett; Mr and Mrs Robert Heber-Percy; Mrs Rosemary Verey; Mr Michael Jessup, Mr Ken Vaughan, Mr George Thompson, Mr Tom Burr and Ms Deana Webb, all of the National Trust; Dr J. M. Naish; Mrs J. Wright; Mrs J. Hignett; Dr and Mrs J. Beviss; Mr Alan Wassell; Marquess and Marchioness of Bath; Dr and Mrs E. A. Nicoll; Mr and Mrs George Lane Fox; Mrs Sybil Spencer; Mr and Mrs Michael de Wend Fenton; Mr Richard Vane; Mr Malcolm Hutcheson; Colonel Slessor; Lord Saye and Sele; Mr Simon Howard; Mr Dennis Hopkins, Mr and Mrs Wilfred Stace; Brigadier Pulverman; Mrs A. J. Woodruff; Mr and the Hon. Mrs A. Heber-Percy.

I would also like to thank the authors, Guy Cooper and Gordon Taylor, for their garden research, and last but not least Wendy Dallas of Weidenfeld and Nicolson, without whose help the editing of the pictures would have been a nightmare.

Clive Boursnell, 1987

⇒ Bibliography ⇐

Ebberston Hall
North Yorkshire

Ebberston Hall is what the French would call a pavillon, a miniature country house built in the eighteenth century. The façade, designed in 1718 by Colen Campbell, is architecturally splendid. At the back, two of the hall's four rooms look up a Yorkshire dale and over the remains of a once very elaborate water garden, also designed on a miniature scale. Nature has overtaken most of the design and all that remains is a pale shadow. Natural springs feed a series of ponds on three levels and flow over a cascade flanked by two stone urns about thirty yards from the house before vanishing underground. Although plans of the original layout survive, it is hard to know whether these water gardens should be re-created as they were or be allowed to stay as they are, in the romantic evening of their existence, black swans and all.

Bailey, Liberty Hyde & Ethel Zoe *Hortus Third* (Macmillan, New York, 1976)

Bruce, Marianne *London Parks & Gardens* (The Pevensey Press, Cambridge, 1986)

Chittenden, Fred J., Editor *The R.H.S. Dictionary of Gardening* (Oxford University Press, 1951)

Coats, Peter *Great Gardens of Britain* (Artus, London, 1977)

Connolly, Cyril & Jerome Zerbe *Les Pavillons* (Hamish Hamilton, London, 1962)

Crowe Sylvia *Garden Design* (Country Life, London, 1965)

Edwards, Paul *English Garden Ornament* (G. Bell & Sons, London)

Fedden, Robin & John Kenworthy-Browne *The Country House Guide*, (Jonathan Cape, London, 1979)

Gardens of England & Wales Open to the Public (The National Gardens Scheme, London, 1986)

Gathorne-Hardy, Robert *Ottoline* (Faber & Faber, London, 1963)

Hinde, Thomas *Stately Gardens of Britain* (Ebury Press, London, 1983)

Hobhouse, Penelope *Private Gardens of England* (Weidenfeld & Nicolson, London, 1986)

Hunt, John Dixon & Peter Willis *The Genius of the Place* (Elek, London, 1975)

Hunt, Peter *The Shell Gardens Book* (Rainbird, London, 1964)

Innes, Mary M. *The Metamorphoses of Ovid* (Penguin, London, 1964)

Jekyll, Gertrude *Wall, Water and Woodland Gardens* (Antique Collectors' Club, 1982) *Garden Ornament* (Country Life/Newnes, London, 1927)

Jellicoe, Goode & Lancaster *The Oxford Companion to Gardens* (Oxford University Press, 1986)

Johnson, Hugh *The Principles of Gardening* (Mitchell Beazley, London, 1979)

Lees-Milne, James *Baroque 1685–1715* (Country Life, London, 1970)

Nicolson, Nigel *The National Trust Book of Great Houses of Britain* (The National Trust & Weidenfeld & Nicolson, London, 1978)

Pearson, Robert, Susane Mitchell & Candida Hunt *The Ordnance Survey Guide to Gardens in Britain* (Newnes, London, 1986)

Perry, Frances *Water Gardens* (Country Life, London, 1938)

Plumptre, George *Collins Book of British Gardens* (Collins, London, 1985)

Readers Digest Encyclopaedia of Garden Plants & Flowers, (Reader's Digest Association, London, 1971)

Stroud, Dorothy *Capability Brown* (Faber & Faber, London, 1975)

Thomas, Graham Stuart *Gardens of The National Trust* (The National Trust/Weidenfeld & Nicolson, London, 1979)

Recreating the Period Garden (Collins, London, 1984)

Tipping, H. Avray *English Gardens* (Country Life, London, 1925)

Wilson, David *Moated Sites* (Shire Publications, Princes Risborough, 1985)

Wilson, Michael *William Kent* (Routledge & Kegan Paul, London, 1984)

➤Authors' Acknowledgments◄

We would like to thank all the owners and trustees of the gardens included in this book, particularly those mentioned in the Photographic Notes; we are grateful for their co-operation and help. We give special thanks to Peter Avery, Emma Brash, James Compton of the Chelsea Physic Garden, Brian Crosby-Hogan, the late Reverend Geoffrey Pollard, John Sandoe and Rosemary Verey, and to Wendy Dallas and Michael Dover of Weidenfeld & Nicolson; finally, and most of all, to Clive Boursnell for his excellent photographs.

❧Index❧